ROUTLEDGE LIBRARY EDITIONS: AGING

Volume 9

DOMICILIARY SERVICES FOR THE ELDERLY

DOMICILIARY SERVICES FOR THE ELDERLY

LIAM CLARKE

LONDON AND NEW YORK

First published in 1984 by Croom Helm

This edition first published in 2024
by Routledge
4 Park Square, Milton Park, Abingdon, Oxon OX14 4RN

and by Routledge
605 Third Avenue, New York, NY 10158

Routledge is an imprint of the Taylor & Francis Group, an informa business

British Library Cataloguing in Publication Data
A catalogue record for this book is available from the British Library

ISBN: 978-1-032-67433-9 (Set)
ISBN: 978-1-032-73267-1 (Volume 9) (hbk)
ISBN: 978-1-032-73270-1 (Volume 9) (pbk)
ISBN: 978-1-003-46340-5 (Volume 9) (ebk)

DOI: 10.4324/9781003463405

Publisher's Note
The publisher has gone to great lengths to ensure the quality of this reprint but points out that some imperfections in the original copies may be apparent.

Disclaimer
The publisher has made every effort to trace copyright holders and would welcome correspondence from those they have been unable to trace.

DOMICILIARY SERVICES FOR THE ELDERLY

Liam Clarke

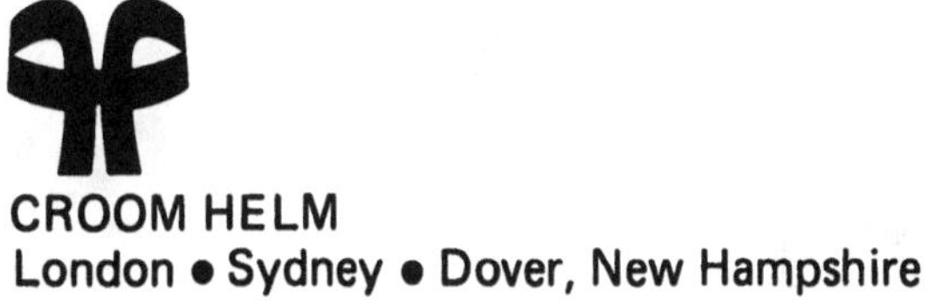
CROOM HELM
London • Sydney • Dover, New Hampshire

Croom Helm Ltd, Provident House, Burrell Row,
Beckenham, Kent BR3 1AT

Croom Helm Australia Pty Ltd, First Floor, 139 King Street,
Sydney, NSW 2001, Australia

Croom Helm, 51 Washington Street,
Dover, New Hampshire, 03820 USA

British Library Cataloguing in Publication Data

Clarke, Liam
Domiciliary services for the elderly.
1. Aged–Services for–Great Britain
I. Title
362.6'3 HV1481.G5

ISBN 0-7099-0756-7

Printed in Great Britain by
Biddles Ltd, Guildford, Surrey

CONTENTS

TABLES AND DIAGRAMS

Tables

Diagrams

ACKNOWLEDGEMENTS

The ideas expressed in this book owe much to many colleagues that I have had the pleasure of working with over many years in the statutory and voluntary social service field and latterly in the education system. I must, however, record certain special debts. My thanks must go to David Phillips of the Department of Sociological Studies, Sheffield University, whose support I valued, particularly his stimulating supervision. This work arises from my post graduate Ph.D. research on the role of the home help, care assistant and community auxiliary nurse, which I am carrying out as a part time student at Sheffield University. I appreciate the valued help of Mrs J. Hazlewood of the Institute of Home Help Organisers who allowed my access to the files of the Institute. I thank Robin Means of the School of Advanced Urban Studies, Bristol University for his criticism and support. I must also acknowledge the support and contributions of the Domiciliary Care Students that I have taught over the past four years. None of the foregoing are responsible for the uses to which I have put their counsels.

My greatest debt is to my wife who, throughout our marriage, has always attempted to awaken in me the confidence to put my ideas on paper whatever the consequences. Without her support and the understanding of my children this work would not have been completed.

Thanks are also due to Mrs Gillian Brown who helped prepare and type the manuscript.

I will be satisfied if, among the readers of this work, there are those who will be sufficiently critical to correct my mistakes. As a qualified social worker, ex social services manager and now senior lecturer in social policy and law, I hope that my domiciliary colleagues do not think that I am disqualified from speculating and reflecting on the future of the Domiciliary Services.

Despite my reliance upon the experiences and advice of many people, I take full responsibility for the opinions expressed and the defects of this work.

Table 1.1 is reproduced with permission of The Royal Society of Health, London.
Table 4.1 is Crown copyright, 1982; reproduced with the permission of the Controller of her Majesty's Stationery Office.
Table 6.2 is reproduced with permission of The Society of St. Vincent de Paul, Ireland.

INTRODUCTION

The ideas expressed in this volume are the product of over 15 years experience of working in the Social Services field. They are the result of the excitement of working for voluntary organisations and the frustrations experienced in a number of bureaucratic Social Service Departments. As a qualified social worker who later qualified in Law, I have become very concerned and disturbed by the restrictions and sometimes deliberate denial of rights imposed by the social work profession upon the elderly. As a Deputy Director of Social Services for four years, I became acutely aware of the low priority given to the needs of the elderly by Social Service Departments. One exception to the rule in many Social Service Departments is the Domiciliary Service Section. Workers in this field have always had the needs of the elderly foremost in their mind. However, they have not had a strong voice in the management of Social Service Departments, unlike field social workers, who since 1972 have had a say in the management of Social Services out of all proportion to their numbers and importance. Domiciliary staff are exploited, taken for granted, overworked, underpaid and have few promotion prospects to higher posts in the Department. They have a right to be angry with their more qualified and status conscious social work colleagues. The Domiciliary Workers' strength is that they put the needs of the client above status or promotion. This strength, however, is also their weakness, they spend very little time in trying to develop their professional identity or organising themselves into a politically motivated body who could speak out against injustices to themselves and their clients.

As a qualified social worker, after much

thought and deliberation, it was painful for me to reach the conclusion that the future care of the elderly would fare better, not in the hands of the social workers, but with domiciliary workers. Domiciliary workers have the motivation, dedication and experience to provide effective and efficient care services for the elderly. My main thesis is that a new service delivery system for the elderly must be developed incorporating the present Domiciliary Service. I hope that, because I foresee only a minor but important part in any new scheme for qualified field social workers, my social work colleagues will not reject my ideas without discussion. Because I have declared my anger at the treatment of the elderly by my profession, I hope it will not be seen as a weakness in my argument, or polemical or lacking in scholarship. The issues I highlight must be discussed. Very few would argue that, in these times of change, the roles of those who work with the elderly, mentally handicapped or mentally ill do not need clarification. Who does what and with whom needs to be researched, discussed and conclusions reached, not based on superior political pressure or status, but on the needs of the client. One issue that is paramount for domiciliary workers concerns the effects of 'patch' and other attempts to provide services at local level. No one has yet examined the effect of social workers leading 'patch' teams compared with say residential or domiciliary staff. The field social worker without discussion has assumed the leadership of these teams, perhaps to the detriment of the service in the long run. What evidence is there to support the field social workers assumption that they are the appropriate people to manage social service (not social work) teams?

There are different forms of decentralisation of which 'patch' is only one, but behind all these proposals to re-organise social service delivery systems lie important questions which must be faced about the frustrations and anxieties of domiciliary care staff. How will these attempts to develop new service delivery systems affect them? Is there any scope for promotion? Can they ever be equal to other professional groups?

One of the strengths of this book, I hope, is that it is written by a social worker. I am not a domiciliary worker 'building an empire'. I also challenge the present Health and Social Service divide, particularly in the area of support to the elderly. For this reason I have included discussion on the home nursing service and the overlap between home helps and in particular community auxiliary nurses.

Chapter one explores the early influences that have helped shape the development of Domiciliary Services for the elderly. The origins of the different groups that now support the elderly are discussed. It becomes clear in the discussion that planning, co-operation and co-ordination of services is a recent phenomenon. Many pressures led to the States' intervention in providing services for the elderly. The changing family structure, the increase in the elderly population and the difficulties caused by the Second World War which also led to the disappearance of the domestic servant. The attempts in the 1960s by the Government to introduce national ten year plans only highlighted the uneven distribution and differing standards of service.

Chapter two addresses itself to the effect upon Domiciliary Service of efforts to re-organise both the Health and Welfare Services in the late 1960s. Many factors led to the demand for a re-organisation of the Social Welfare Services, not least the pressure by General Practitioners to head Domiciliary Teams. This pressure led to the collapse of the Local Authority Health Departments. The control of Mental Welfare and Domiciliary Social Services all became part of the new Social Service Departments in 1972. Domiciliary Nursing Services became part of the new Health Authorities in 1974. The chapter also discusses the uncertainty which was in the minds of Domiciliary Care Staff at that time as to whether they were Health or Social Service oriented. The matter was settled for them by the decision to place their service in the Social Service Departments, despite arguments from medical and nursing pressure groups. The role of the family in looking after the elderly since 1948 is examined as is the inability of the Voluntary Organisations to provide domiciliary services. The difficulties faced by families and Voluntary Organisations to support the elderly or provide services, led Local Authorities to argue for powers to support the family and replace Voluntary Organisations. The result was the 1962 National Assistant Amendment Act and the 1968 Health Services and Public Health Act. By the beginning of 1980 it was all too clear that the rhetoric of various Governments, concerning services for the elderly, had not been translated into concrete services. Services in fact were being cut or restricted.

Chapter three looks at the effect of the placement of Domiciliary Services in the Social Service Departments and the Domiciliary Nursing Services in the Health Authorities. This split in services led to unco-ordinated planning and un-even distribution of services. The effect of the re-awakening of concern about demographic changes and the growing restrictions on public expenditure are examined. 1948 to 1980 was not a continuum of growing appreciation of Domiciliary Services. In the late sixties, people argued that services should be generally available to the elderly, but by the late seventies, Governments stressed the need for priorities and value for money. Detailed investigation of demand for services was the order of the day. Emphasis is now care by the community which is seen by many as a ploy or excuse to cut services, or at least not develop them and so place the responsibility for care upon the family or voluntary groups or private concerns.

How the policies discussed in chapter three have affected the services in the 1980s is examined in chapters four and five. Many new innovations are discussed and their effect upon differing services is highlighted. Questions about the Home Help Service and the overlap with the home nursing service are touched upon as is the important question of payment for the Home Help Service. The Health Service is free, home helps are usually charged for. Who, therefore, has the right to say that a client should have one service which is free as against another for which the client may have to pay. Many of the new schemes discussed also raise questions about the role confusion and overlap between the Home Help and Community Nursing Service, particularly the auxiliary nurse. There is confusion in both the minds of staff and clients. Much work needs to be done in this area if an efficient and effective service is to be offered to clients. The discussion of new schemes in this chapter give the opportunity to develop the general themes of the previous chapters. I argue strongly about the effects of the Health - Social Service divide and the effect upon clients and services.

Chapter six concerns itself with an analysis of Domiciliary Services in Ireland and Sweden, which allows me to draw upon the best aspects of both services and examine what lessons could be learned and applied to the services in Britain. Ireland was selected because the Domiciliary Services are relatively new provisions. Many of the lessons learned from Europe were implemented. There is no split between Health and Social Service provision and there is much co-operation between State and Voluntary Organisations in the provision of services. Both the Irish and Swedish Governments have set up national bodies to co-ordinate and innovate new services for the elderly. In Sweden the Domiciliary Services for the elderly are very well developed, perhaps the best in the World. The Domiciliary Organiser manages many of the services for the elderly which, in Britain, are the responsibility of various agencies, such as home helps, residential care, transport, day care and many others. The total social care needs of the elderly are, therefore, assessed by one person who is able to allocate resources as necessary. How the two Countries are meeting the needs of the elderly are outlined and suggestions made as to how Britain could implement some of the concepts discussed.

One of the main reasons why the Domiciliary Services are of such a low status in the eyes of many professions in Britain is their inadequate training opportunities and lack of qualified staff. Much of the fault for this situation can be laid at the door of both the Institute of Home Help Organisers and their inability to co-operate with any training scheme that leans toward 'social work' and CCETSW, the body responsible for all training in the Social Services field, to respond to the needs of Domiciliary Care Staff. The introduction of the Certificate in Social Service as a qualification for all staff except field social workers has only added fuel to the fire. Many see the qualification as second rate and an attempt by qualified field social workers to control the profession. The need for a clear distinction between training needs of Organisers and care staff, such as home helps, is not necessary because I believe there should be no barriers between progression from home help to organiser, middle manager and perhaps one day to Director of Social Services. Along side any change in service delivery must go a training structure which will meet the needs of the staff. I propose the setting up of a new training council for workers in the field of caring for the elderly. This may be a naive proposal in view of the stranglehold of CCETSW on Social Service training but one, nevertheless, that should be considered.

The present unstructured and divisive system of training and service delivery, is a major obstacle to the delivery of a comprehensive programme of community care to the elderly. The need for co-operation by means of interdisciplinary structure is important not only from the viewpoint of the client, but also because it avoids costly and time wasting duplication of services and mistakes.

Chapter eight concerns the argument for a new service delivery system for supporting the elderly in the community. I am aware of the complexity of service delivery in Social Service Departments. Many hide behind this complexity and use it as an excuse for not changing or examining the power structure of the department. I argue that both residential care and qualified field social workers have failed the elderly. A new concept of service delivery is outlined, based upon the needs of clients not the needs of professional groups. My proposals are, that all services for the elderly should be brought together under one roof, a neighbourhood centre. These suggestions are not far from those made by Meacher in the 1970s but go further in comprehensiveness and argue for client and worker participation in the control of the service. Many have argued for client participation in the provision of services, but most professionals do not go far enough. They do not object to clients advising or serving on committees not having voting rights as is present where representatives of Voluntary Organisations are co-opted on to Social Service Committees. Even Hadley and Hatch, who believe in consumer participation, do not go very far in their proposals. In 1981 in their book 'Social Welfare and the Failure of the State' they argue that "Clients should have the right to information on its management and to make representations concerning the operations of the service", I go much further in relation to my scheme for the elderly and argue that they should have the right to representation on any management structure which makes decisions about their service or their future. Thus both clients, the worker and the local community, in the form of the elected member, would make policy decisions. Would professionals allow this?

Ask most old people what they think old age is about and they will reply with a blank stare. After a lifetime of work, service to the community and rearing families they continue to feel that they should be some use to society, but they are largely condemned to passivity. Since the elderly have contributed so much to society they are entitled to at least the same rights as other sections of the community. Care of the aged is not a matter of charity or second best, but of human dignity and social justice. The elderly in our society suffer deplorable social injustices and lack of medical and social care programmes. On the other hand, old age does not mean a period of special privileges. Old people have the same duties as the rest of society, that is the obligation to look after themselves whenever they are able to do so and to take part and contribute to the community they live in. The approach of society towards the elderly, particularly the elderly infirm, is one of the most important challenges facing society. However, in the long term, it is desirable to concentrate on ways in which the incidence of illness in the aged can be lowered and life made easier, safer and more challenging for them in the community and in their own homes. This will not only bring economic benefits to the community, but will also materially raise the quality of life for the elderly.

Most of us today are destined to grow old and the aged of today hold up the mirror of the future to the young and middle aged who will themselves be the aged of tomorrow. Old age is a reality which concerns everyone and to neglect its problems spells suffering and misery to those who have to bear the indignities and deprivations that will come with advancing years. Their present is our future.

Chapter One

THE EARLY DEVELOPMENT OF DOMICILIARY SERVICES

At the beginning of this century the prospects for those past earning and nearing old age were grim indeed. For many old people who could not live on the charity of friends or relations, the only support was the workhouse. Here they lived uprooted from their past, as partial prisoners in uniform with very little freedom, no personal possessions and with a complete loss of individuality.

The 1908 Old Age Pensions Act and the 1925 Contributory Pensions Act gave many of the elderly their freedom but a lot found that financial support was by no means all. The provisions of the 1908 and 1925 Acts did however lead to a reduction in the number of old people relying on Poor Law relief[1] but if these financial supports failed, the only course open to the elderly was to live alone in the community, to live with relatives or in someone elses house as a lodger. For many there was no choice but to enter the workhouse.

Domiciliary services for the elderly were virtually non existant. Any that there were have been poorly documented. Later I shall examine the Report of The Royal Commission on the Poor Law of 1909[2] to see what it had to say about the state of the elderly sick and infirm. As the century progressed welfare and health services for the elderly began to consume more and more of the Health and Welfare budget. The lack of research into domiciliary care of the elderly was, up to 1970, only too apparent to those who needed information to plan and develop services.[3] It is only in the last fifteen years that research into domiciliary home nursing has begun.[4]

It is one of the objectives of a domiciliary service to see that those extra years are happy ones and not years of pain, isolation, suffering and loss of individualism and freedom. The ability of schemes to meet this objective has always differed. The standard of care varied at the beginning of the century and today still varies from agency to agency and authority to authority.[5] The beginning of modern day services can be traced to voluntary agencies in the late 19th century.[6] The concern about the lack of community care and health facilities for the sick and elderly infirm is evident from the Majority and Minority reports of the 1909 Poor Law Committee. One of the results of the publication of the report was to persuade the nation that poverty and sickness were not a social crime. It was argued that poverty could be the result of economic forces, lack of resources or information in times of illness, or at certain stages of life such as old age, the birth of children, or unemployment.

Dr McVail in his report on Poor Law Medical Relief in England and Wales, to the committee, forsaw the desperate need for domiciliary services particularly for the sick and infirm elderly. He argued the need for domiciliary nurses, the lack of whom he said was "serious in the present system of poor law relief". He also argued for a service, very much like the present day home help service, as a support to the medical and nursing services "what many paupers need is a little skilled guidance in tending chronic ailments and in others it is house keeping rather than nursing that is wanted, the washing and cleansing of an aged man or woman, attention to body and bed clothing, the keeping of the house fresh and clean".[7] The minority report gave many examples of inadequate community facilities for the elderly. It pointed out that it was rare "for the Guardians to make any sort of provision for nursing the outdoor sick poor". One example which typified the others was that of an old man in very poor health. "This is the case of a man dying of cancer in the throat. We found the door locked, and but for a kindly neighbour who opened a window and found the key, we could not have got in, the man being quite alone, hardly able to speak, and horribly ill. The house was poor, a daughter earns 9s a week the only regular income, and the rent is 4s2d. The old wife had gone to a neighbour where she would earn 4d by minding the house".[8] This example of an old person and his family's suffering is one where the provisions of the 1908 and 1925 Pensions Acts could have helped. How could help in the community be offered?

Some argued for "the employment of respectable women to thoroughly clean and keep clean the houses of the poor where there is sickness in the house". Others who gave evidence however felt that the family should be encouraged to help out with these tasks. "Do you think there is any room for further development in the shape of nursing assistants, whose job would be simply to keep the home clean in such cases? - No I think not, it is far better that friends and relations should help each other".[9]

Some gave evidence to the committee that people had actually died because of the lack of nursing or other domiciliary support in the community. Many doctors stated that their job was made ineffective by the lack of domiciliary services "There is no doubt in my mind but that medical assistance to the poor is seriously affected by the complete absence of any organised scheme for the proper nursing of the patients in their own houses".[10] The Majority report was very critical of the Poor Law Guardians for having failed to provide a nursing service to the sick and infirm under the Outdoor Nursing Order 1892. They recommended that the Public Assistance Authority appoint outdoor nurses and also that "immediate steps should be taken for the organisation of a satisfactory system of nursing, or attendance, for the outdoor sick poor".[11] The history of organised community nursing goes back to 1859 when William Rathbourn engaged a Mrs Robinson to nurse his wife who was ill at home. He was so impressed by her services he engaged her to nurse the sick in the community in poor districts of Liverpool. The work of the community nursing service, by 1900, called The District Nursing Services, was well established in most areas but the number and standard varied.

The Government by 1908 began to recognise the separate needs of the elderly by the introduction of pensions but until 1944 very little else was done for the elderly except in the area of housing. Local Authorities were given powers to subsidise housing for the elderly in 1936. The responsibility for the elderly in workhouses was transfered to Local County and County Boroughs in 1929. The first major advance in community care of the elderly came in 1944 not as a result of concern by the community or professions but as a direct result of economic and social problems brought about by war. The National Old Peoples Welfare Council had been established in 1940 to encourage and co-ordinate local welfare committees for the elderly to help overcome the problems brought about by the plight of the increasing numbers of the elderly affected by the war. By 1961 there were 1,600 local committees in England and Wales.

To help in time of stress or help with household chores some families could in 1939 still rely on private domestic servants. Estimates put the number of private domestic servants in 1939 at 159,000.[12] During the war the mobilization of men and women left very few able people who could enter domestic service or look after the elderly. By 1940 the armed forces had enlisted 2.25 million men and by 1944 4.5 million or 30 per cent of the working male population. This meant that there were 4.5 million men living away from home unable to help or look after the needs of aged relatives. The later mobilization of women exacerbated this situation as did the evacuation of families which also brought about a very steep reduction in domestic labour of about 75 per cent less than before the war. This disruption in family life came about just as the number of elderly in the population was on the increase. It was pointed out by Ferguson and Fitzgerald[13] "what the family and neighbourhood could no longer do for themselves the state had to help them to do. The social services therefore, far from being reduced in war time had to be expanded. To most people in 1939 it would have seemed scarcely credible that war should prove an agent of great social advance". The Government had to step in and fill the gaps in the informal and formal caring systems left by the break up of families, decrease in domestic servants and problems of mobilization.

The disappearing domestic servant had been a cause of concern to the Government since the end of the 19th century. The decline was highlighted in a report in 1919[14] which had examined the problems brought about by changes in attitude to the work as a result of the first world war. The first war had it seemed the same effect upon domestic labour as the second. To examine the problems after the second war two Government committees were set up. One to examine the wages and conditions of domestic workers in schools and hospitals and the second to examine the post war organisation of private domestic service.[15]

A report had previously been published which had suggested the provision of a domiciliary service for poor families with a sick member.[16] The report drew attention to the need for consideration of the problems experienced by the large number of families who could not afford to employ someone to do domestic work in the home regularly, but who urgently needed assistance in time of incapacity through illness or other causes. The report pointed out that because of the lack of domiciliary services, the whole machinery the working woman broke down during illness, but that she continued to perform her household tasks even when she was totally unfit. The resulting suffering and ill health it was suggested might have been avoided if there had been a system of 'home helps' which the committee felt should have been provided by Local Authorities. This service, if it had been supported at that time by the Government, would have been a tremendous help to the large number of elderly persons who lived with families and also those females in households who had to carry out tasks in good or bad health. Over 55 per cent of the elderly in the mid 1940's lived with their families.[17] Many of these would have lost the support of families and friends for a time because of mobilization of their sons and daughters.

The Government, concerned at the position of the elderly sick and infirm who were unable to obtain a hospital bed or help in the home, drew the attention of Local Health and Welfare Authorities in 1944 to Defence Regulation 68E which enabled them to extend the domiciliary services they provided to mothers and children to the elderly and infirm.[18] This regulation was in part a response to the problems brought about by the war, the changing family structure, the lack of hospital beds for the elderly and the changes in the domestic servant situation.

The fall in the distribution of different age groups in society reflected the fall in family size. In 1851, 35 per cent of the population was between 0-14 years of age, 60 per cent 15-64 years and only 5 per cent were over 65 years of age. By 1951 however this situation had changed so that 11 per cent of the population were in the 0-14 age group, 67 per cent in the 15-64 age group and over 11 per cent in the 65 plus group. The percentage of children in the population fell from 35 per cent in 1851 to 22 per cent in 1951 whereas the percentage of elderly rose from 5 per cent in 1911 to 11 in 1951. If the number of men over 65 and women over 60 is considered the increase is even more dramatic, 7 per cent of the population in 1911 to 14 per cent in 1951. The elderly therefore formed 1 in 15 of the population. The total number of elderly had risen from one million in 1851 to over six and a half million in 1951.[19] This change in the structure of society contributed to the social and economic problems of the elderly brought about during and after the war.

In 1942 The Ministry of Health, concerned at the plight of the elderly, began to enquire into the extent of arrangements made by Local Authorities to provide domiciliary service schemes to help them. It was found that only just over half had schemes, and many that did not, laid the blame on their inability to recruit staff.

Because of the difficulty in recruiting domiciliary staff the Ministry of Labour gave the same high priority to their recruitment as to domestic service in hospitals and also encouraged suitable persons to take up the work.[20]

As Local Authorities had only power to provide a domiciliary service to maternity cases, widening the criteria to allow them to offer the service to the elderly was an obvious way to help the elderly. The problems caused by the war and the declining domestic service industry made it imperative that some form of domiciliary help was offered. Powers were given to Local Authorities to provide such domiciliary services as home helps to the elderly in 1944. Advice was issued in Ministry of Health Circular 179/44 which stated the Government's concern at the position of the elderly sick and infirm unable to obtain domestic help and Local Authorities were asked to submit schemes for the Minister's approval, only after they were satisfied of the need for such a service in their area. The Authorities were allowed to appoint domestic helps, to arrange their payment and to recover part of the costs from the clients or their families.[21]

During 1945 and 1946 a number of schemes became operational and were administered alongside the maternity home help schemes. The chief objective of the service to the elderly was to enable them to stay at home at times of illness or infirmity "thereby reserving beds in hospital for the most urgent cases". Some local authorities managed to service themselves and others allowed voluntary agencies to do so on their behalf, paying them the running costs of the service. Voluntary Organisations also began to meet the needs of the elderly by providing Meals on Wheels and District Nursing Services.[22]

The role of voluntary organisations must not be

underestimated when looking at the development of services for the elderly. Voluntary organisations had throughout the centuries provided and pioneered services for the sick and infirm. Since 1949 the Minister of Health had encouraged the use of voluntary agencies by local authorities, by allowing them to make contributions to their funds.[23] Voluntary organisations pioneered the fostering of old people with families, friendly visiting and home help schemes. Exeter Council of Social Services received grants in 1951 to set up a domiciliary old persons housework scheme. This scheme allowed for helpers to undertake shopping, cooking, washing clothes, washing the old person, collecting pensions, collecting Gin and Cider, taking elderly people to the seaside and many more tasks.[24] Chiropody services were not encouraged until the Government lifted its restriction on the service in 1959.[25] Local Authorities were encouraged by the Ministry to rectify the unevenness of the spread of Voluntary Services in 1962 and later that same year to take into account the services of voluntary agencies when submitting ten year plans to the Minister.[26]

Many Authorities however failed to establish any kind of home help service putting forward the problems of recruiting staff. Guidance was issued to Authorities in 1946 following an investigation into their problems.[27] Two successful schemes were outlined and lessons drawn from their success and organisation. It was concluded that some schemes were successful because they were managed by full time organisers who devoted their whole time to the schemes. The view of the Minister was that full time organisers were essential, which was contrary to earlier advice.

The difficulties of recruitment experienced by some Authorities, the Minister hoped to overcome by implementing in part the recommendations of the Report on Post War Organisation of Domestic Service which suggested the setting up of a National Institute of Houseworkers which would train domestics and home helps.[28] The objective of the Institute was "to act as a National or central organisation throughout the United Kingdom for increasing the supply of domestic workers and for that purpose to provide a centre for research into all questions relating to the supply and demand for such workers". Local Authorities used the services of the Institute to train their staff, recognised the Diploma of the Institute and paid an additional hourly rate of pay to holders of the qualification.[29]

As very little was written about services for the elderly or the domiciliary needs of the elderly it is difficult to ascertain the state of the service before the operation of the National Health Service. In 1946 the Council of The British Medical Association appointed a committee to look into the provision for the care and treatment of the elderly sick and infirm. This report[30] laid too much emphasis on institutional care for the aged and the responsibility of the domiciliary services was overlooked in favour of geriatric services in institutions, "It was only when it was realised that the hospitals were not in a position to provide the necessary number of staffed beds that a period of retrenchment was necessary. It then became a matter of urgency to investigate not only how to keep old people at home but how to look after them adequately".[31] By 1945 only 19 Local Authorities had domiciliary care schemes and only 2 were considered successful. Only 2 research studies give up any clues as to the state or needs of the elderly pre 1948. Rowntree surveyed 7 areas in England and Wales in 1946 to ascertain the needs of the elderly and the services needed to support them.[32] He found that just over 62 per cent of men and nearly 40 per cent of women were married. 30.2 per cent of men were widowed and over 48 per cent of women. Only 7 per cent of men were single and just over 11 per cent of women. Rowntree found that over 23 per cent of the elderly lived alone. By 1979 this figure had risen to 45 per cent for females and 18 per cent for men. This report and a later one by Sheldon in 1948 'The Social Medicine of Old Age' gave a vivid picture of the state of services. The surveys show all too clearly the lack of domiciliary services and that the strains and problems of old age bore no relation to class or income. The reports showed that the elderly who were sick and infirm became a burden on their families but not one that was necessarily resented. Fifty nine per cent of old people lived with their families. When one of the family became ill in most cases it was the female members of the family who did the nursing. Only in 10 per cent of cases did a male member of the household nurse a sick member. Nearly 40 per cent of the elderly were nursed by their daughters. To help with these duties over 18 per cent would have welcomed nursing help and 22 per cent would have liked some form of domestic help.[33] Sheldon also pointed out special problems faced by spouses nursing their partners in their last illness and men who had to nurse illness. The elderly persons extra source of help during illness came from the nursing service, 11 per cent compared to 13 per cent receiving domestic help. Over 57 per cent received no extra support during illness. Sheldon also looked at the extra help that families requested but did not optain. Over 13 per cent requested nursing help and over 17 per cent asked for domestic support. This report all too clearly pointed to the need for an increase in the provision of domiciliary home help and nursing services to help families. The extra nursing and domestic help was most needed by the elderly. It was clear from the reports that many old people living alone needed help, especially old men living alone and those of both sexes over 80 years of age. The supply of nursing and domestic support by the health and welfare authorities fell far short of what was needed to meet existing needs and in some parts of the country it was non existant. Recruitment problems caused some of these difficulties but in areas like London no such problems existed. The serious shortage of nurses and particularly those trained in working with the elderly was a most serious problem. In Mid Rhondda for example there was only one district nurse for a population of over 30,000 and she was not provided with any form of transport. In most authorities urgent applications for nursing help had to be refused because of the shortage of staff.

The social value of domiciliary services particularly domestic and Meals on Wheels services had been proved by 1948. The Minister recognised this by making them a feature of the new National Health Service. The home help service was extended to the elderly, sick and infirm, handicapped and maternity cases.[34] Some authorities had operated schemes for some time. In 1948 the City of Coventry had 50 full time home helps who were paid 1s8d per hour plus travelling expenses, they got no paid holidays, sick pay or superannuation. In contrast, Worcester City had 7 full time and 7 part time staff who were paid £3 11s 6d for a 48 hour week, were allowed a holiday with pay and sick pay which was also the situation in Salford, South Shields, Lancashire and Sheffield but Northumberland operated the same scheme as Coventry and Doncaster.[35]

Section 25 of the National Health Service Act 1948 placed a duty on Local Health Authorities to provide nurses to attend upon persons in their own home free of charge. In the domiciliary home help service the Minister again encouraged the appointment of full time organisers to recruit, train staff and administer schemes. Transport was to be provided for organisers and training given. In rural areas, authorities were advised to co-operate with voluntary organisations in providing the service or in organising "mutual neighbour-to-neighbour agreement for reciprocal help".

Those who organised and managed the service for the elderly saw them as a vital support to the medical and nursing services, providing care where there was no hospital bed or facilitating early discharge from hospital. The service was mainly a female occupation.[36] By 1951 however men had made a valuable contribution to the service "male home helps are making their appearance in this area and have proved eminently satisfactory. The only obstacle to extending their employment is prejudice - mainly from male patients".[37]

No guidelines were laid down by the Minister as to the number of nurses or home helps to be employed. In London one home help per 1,500 of the population was thought necessary. However the service was not seen as a rehabilitative one. At the first conference organised by the W.V.S. in 1948 for Home Help Organisers on domiciliary services, Mrs Ritchley, a welfare officer, spoke of the absolute dependency of many old people on meals on wheels and home help. Yet at an earlier national conference in 1947 S. F. Wilkinson a senior civil servant in the Ministry of Health had argued that the elderly should not automatically be considered for domiciliary services. His remarks cast doubt upon the enthusiasm of the Ministry to make available domiciliary services to the elderly. Others saw the service as supporting the Health Visitor and home nurse but some envisaged the service as a new development standing in its own right and a new career for women. By 1956 the high cost of providing domiciliary services for the elderly was causing concern to Central Government and Local Authorities. To examine the financial and economic pressures caused by this high expenditure a committee was set up with particular reference to look at the cost of The National Health Service. The committee examined the problems caused by the increasing number of old age persons and the resulting problems caused in the areas of pensions and income schemes for the elderly. The committee did also examine the situation in respect of the problems of providing hospital beds and domiciliary care. The report found that by 1953 local authorities had wide powers to provide such services as home nursing, care and after care of the elderly, domestic help, meals on wheels, residential accommodation and sheltered housing for the elderly. The cost of the home nursing service was £2 million pounds, the home help service cost the same. These services were essential if old people were to be kept active in their own homes. The committee found, as other research had also, that domiciliary services such as domestic help, nurses, health visiting, laundry facilities, chiropody and meals varied in the quality and quantity of service delivery across the country.[38] An argument was made for a swing of finance away from residential care to services which would help old people to stay at home longer "which would be conducive to the happiness of the old people enabling them to remain active members of the community and might well be cheaper".[39] The National Corporation for the Care of Old People in 1956 argued that to keep old people at home and provide domiciliary services would cost more than a hospital bed but we still have the myth of cheap community care with us today.[40] Also recognised by the committee was the confusion and inefficiency caused by the number of staff who visited the elderly delivering different services some times from the same department. Co-ordination was called for so as to eliminate waste in the health and welfare services. Also called for was co-operation between the different branches of the medical profession.[41] An earlier committee had commented upon this problem of lack of co-ordination but had recognised that the National Health Service was so large a concern that perfect co-ordination was impossible and unreasonable to expect.[42] However, this argument may have had something to do with the medical profession's reluctance to accept central control rather than the size of the service. A later committee on the cost of the National Health Service recommended a combined Health and Welfare committee to manage the service for the elderly, improve efficiency and cut down costs. This again was seen by some as an attempt by the medical profession to gain control of such welfare services as social work, residential provision and day care services managed by a lay welfare officer.[43] The division between hospital and local authority services was a much larger concern to the committee in relation to services to the elderly, as was the lack of central Government finance which they pointed out was an obstacle to the smooth development of services which in the long run might even distort the pattern of services.

A great deal of evidence was presented to the committee on the problems of service delivery to the elderly since 1948. Local Authorities argued that most of them could be solved if there was one authority responsible for the management of both hospital and local health and welfare services.

In Exeter in 1951 one voluntary worker reported that she had to call in, to an old person, no less than 16 different agencies to provide services to an 84 year old.[44] The committee however favoured the argument of lack of services as the major problem and recognised that modern methods of geriatric treatment would reduce the numbers of elderly who would be retained in hospital thus causing more strain on the community services. Chalk in 1951 had showed the value of domiciliary services when he reported that in his local authority at least 9 per cent of hospitalised elderly patients were discharged early into the community because of the availability of adequate support services.[45] To facilitate this early discharge from hospital the Government called for more and better rehabilitation services for hospital patients who were elderly and better co-operation between hospital and community care services.

What was the state of domiciliary service delivery at this time? By the end of 1949 all authorities in England and Wales had some form of domiciliary service for the elderly but because of financial constraints the services were underdeveloped and unable to meet the demands of the elderly population at that time.[46] In Dewsbury in 1948 over 36 per cent of the home help service was allocated to the elderly and 40 per cent of home nursing. This had increased in the home nursing division to over 44 per cent in 1953 and over 50 per cent of the home help service by 1953 was allocated to the elderly. By 1954 this proportion had reached 75 per cent.[47] Many of the domiciliary services were managed by voluntary organisations on behalf of the local authorities. In London 32 voluntary Nursing Organisations were co-ordinated by a Central Council for District Nursing which was responsible for a service which covered 117 square miles and served a population of over 3,400,000.[48]

In the county of Kent the increase in the numbers receiving domiciliary services particularly the home help service rose from 1,100 clients per week in 1947 to 4,200 per week in 1956.[49] Despite financial constraints there was a considerable increase in service in some areas of the country. In London the service had grown from 3,159,728 hours worked in 1950 in the home help service to nearly 5 million in 1957 (see Table 1.1). In 1957 there was 29 organisers, 41 assistant organisers and 39 clerks and each organiser was responsible for the management of a group of home helps which varied in number from 60 to 350 per organiser. The service used male helps and found them invaluable. A night service also operated as did a weekend and bank holiday service.[50]

Table 1.1: Growth of L.C.C. home help service 1949-1957

Year	Cases	Hours	Average Hours per Client per Year
1950	25,805	3.159,729	122.4
1951	26,542	3,441,152	129.6
1952	27,896	3,834,688	137.4
1953	30,335	4,269,408	140.7
1954	32,503	4,601,168	141.5
1955	34,785	4,660,600	133.9
1956	34,557	4,779,600	138.3
1957	35,737	4,896,000	137.0

Adapted from RSH Journal No 6, Vol 78 The Contribution of the Home Help Organiser to the Welfare of the Aged, Nepean-Gubbins 1958

Not all Medical Officers who were usually managers of the service, were in agreement with the philosophy of community care. Some argued against it and also against state involvement in the provision of domiciliary service "with its bureaucratic control and its official attitude".[51] Others felt that the pendulum of community care had swung too far in favour of keeping the elderly in the community. The Government, because of pressure from both houses of parliament, the press and professional groups, called for co-operation and co-ordination between hospital, voluntary and statutory services.[52] These un co-ordinated services it was argued allowed both those who were helped and the helper to 'cheat' the system. What form this cheating took was not defined but this view was held particularly by the medical press. The medical profession did however argue for better co-operation and analysis of the domiciliary services "the evident gratitude of so many of those helped by the home help service must not, however, blind us to the economic realities of the times, to the need for a constructive analysis of its working and a steady improvement in its organisation".[53] Some authorities began to research and analyse the services to manage them more effectively. One report is perhaps outstanding in that it emphasised the lack of knowledge of the actual needs of the elderly in the community and the relationship between different services and their effect on demand. The report by Chalk and Benjamin looked at the home help service of the Greater London Council in 1951. Earlier Benjamin had looked at the home nursing service and reported an increase in visits from 970,000 to 37,000 patients in 1946 to 1,086,226 visits to 43,000 patients in 1949 which was in fact a drop in the average number of visits to each client from 26 visits per year to 25 visits per year. This increased demand for the service was linked to the increasing number of aged and chronic sick patients who, if beds had been available, would have been looked after in hospital. Some argued that the shortage in domiciliary services was because the elderly were unwilling to relinquish them, making them unnecessarily and increasingly dependent upon them. As a result of this argument many Local Health Authorities reviewed their domiciliary services to assess their value to the elderly.

No survey of value into the social and medical needs of the elderly was available until 1957. This survey found that what the elderly most needed in order of priority was laundry services, home help, change of accommodation, meals on wheels, social visiting and lastly medical attention.[54] Lord Amulreea,[55] consultant geriatrician, had argued for better housing and domiciliary services in 1956 and some very imaginative schemes were developed by Health and Welfare Authorities despite problems with recruitment of staff and lack of finance. Family help and night attendant schemes were operating in some 50 local authorities by 1953. Kent County Council had started the night attendant scheme because of the many old people needing help at night or evenings when the more conventional services had closed for the day. The service provided help to the bed ridden elderly, with their preparation for the night, and to support ill persons who lived alone with or without a relative. The managers of this scheme were unable to evaluate its effectiveness in keeping old people out of residential or hospital care because of the shortage of these residential facilities.[56] Despite this lack of evaluation of the effectiveness of schemes, the Ministry of Health in 1953 was praising schemes saying they were of "inestimable value" in keeping old people independent.

The most frequent support in the home in the early 1950s was not from relatives but from home helps.[57] Old people were visited infrequently and a large percentage had no visits by relatives, friends or statutory services. This situation existed despite the encouragement of the Minister to Local Authorities to support and form Old Peoples Welfare Committees to organise and develop services for the elderly.[58] Despite this underdevelopment, lack of services and calls for the extension of schemes for the elderly in the community, some voices still argued for the status quo "It is difficult to avoid the conclusion that the community is already saturated with the domestic care of the old people". Calls were made for increases in such domiciliary services as Laundry which had been ranked as the number one by the elderly in Scotland by Gordon in 1957. It was felt that washing of clothes, sheets etc. placed a great strain upon the elderly particularly those over 70 years of age.[59] Only six authorities were by 1953 providing a laundry service but by 1956 this service was being increased to allow home helps to do other jobs in the persons home. Some Authorities like Rotherham had a well developed laundry service which is today one of the most advanced in the country having its own purpose built centre. By 1961 17 of 19 authorities surveyed by the Minister were providing a laundry service.[60] Even today some areas fall down badly when it comes to provision of laundry services "in some parts of the country the service is absolutely abysmal and in some authorities laundry waiting lists are so full that no one can get a service unless a customer dies".[61]

Advice by the Minister in 1957 crystallized for some the ideas and concepts of a well developed domiciliary service which they saw as having been operated by few authorities over the years. This advice concerned an extension of the role of domiciliary services. "As Authorities will know, there has been in the last few years a great increase in the proportion of time devoted by the Home Help service to the care of the aged, as the value of the contribution which the service can make to help them to continue to live in their own homes has been increasingly recognised. As the experience of progressive Authorities has shown the value of this service can still be further enhanced if it is imaginatively planned, with due regard, for example, to the times at which the old person most needs assistance (may be evening attendance) and to the type of help most required, which may extend beyond purely domestic help with cleaning and the preparation of meals to such things as friendly guidance in personal matters and in some cases to help with the toilet and in hygiene".[62] By 1960 Home Nurses and home helps were the most widely known domiciliary services, the least known was chiropody.[63] Home Nurses in 1960 paid 23 million visits to patients in their own homes of which over half were to elderly patients over 65 years of age. The number of nurses employed had risen from 7,000 in 1948 to over 10,000 in 1960. Nursing agencies varied in the intensity and duration of their services. Nurses tended to visit their patients daily for short periods and stopped attending when their services were no longer required. Fourteen per cent of their caseload were elderly but this had risen to over 50 per cent by 1966.[64] There was still a universal shortage of home helps, the number employed had risen from 11,000 in 1948 to 49,000 in 1960. The number of households visited had risen from 139,000 in 1949 to 312,000 in 1960. This statistic however hid a drop in the average number of visits to clients from 12 per year to about 6 per year in 1960. We can see that the service was far from keeping up with demand. Home Helps and meals on wheels only withdrew their service on the death of a client or admission to care. A survey of the over eighties in 1960 called for priority for the domiciliary services and for them to be provided at an early stage of the elderly person's illness or need. These services should also have encouraged the old person to participate in activities in the community. One of the main problems then, and is still today, is the lack of awareness of the elderly of the services available to them. The services surveyed were found to be so inadequate that "prevention in the sense of having as its primary objective to avoid undue deterioration and ultimate breakdown could hardly be said to exist".[65]

By 1961 the policy of Central Government was to provide domiciliary services to support the increasing number of elderly people living in the community and to fill any gaps in the service as quickly as resources would permit. The stated objective of Ministerial policy was to encourage and help the elderly in their own homes as long as practicable.[66] The Conservative Government had been in power for over 11 years by 1963 and critics put forward that neither they or the previous Labour administration had done very much to help the elderly or meet their needs.[67] Information on which to plan services was not available in the early 1960s and because of this lack of basic information a clear picture was not then available of the needs of the elderly. The Government's request for Authorities to submit 10 year plans was a welcome start to bring together the necessary information upon which to begin to build services.

Enoch Powell, the then Minister for Health, in 1961 requested Health Boards to formulate long term plans, which were published in 1962. This publication was circulated to local authorities as the report had put forward that it was "complementary to the expected development of the service for prevention and care in the community and a continued expansion of these services had been taken into account in the assessment of the hospital provision to be aimed at. It follows that the local authorities services need to plan for the same period ahead as the hospital services". The Hospital plan laid emphasis on the principal of community care "the aim will be to provide care at home and in the community for all who do not require the special types of diagnosis and treatment only a hospital can provide.[68] Local Authority plans were to be examined in the light of these statements of intent of helping the elderly, in particular in the community with the support of medical and domiciliary services. The average length of stay for the over 65 in hospital beds had fallen in 1967 from 1962 from 34 to 28 days for men and 45 to 42 days for women.[69] The aim of the Local Authority 10 year plan was to provide a "nationwide picture of the developments as they are at present envisaged and an attempt to set them within the context of national purposes and common standards".

The 1963 plans were revised in 1964 and again in 1966 when they were discontinued. These plans and revisions were criticised by academics and local authority staff alike.[70] It was difficult to draw conclusions from the published figures because no guidance had been given to authorities on the interpretation of figures or level of client need. In some authorities the appropriate staff were involved in the drawing up of the plans, in others, staff , such as Home Help Organisers or Superintendant Nurses, were not involved or given appropriate guidance on how to complete the plans and in some areas no involvement of voluntary agencies was encouraged.[71] The plans, if they could be called that, were just intentions of the Authorities, not based on any objective research into community needs. Despite the obvious needs thrown up by this exercise, Local Authorities still saw services for the elderly as separate and not dependent upon each other.[72] There was however, some research on which to base tentative plans or projections for services for the elderly. Townsend's survey of the elderly in 1957 had shown the need for more domiciliary services for the elderly to just meet existing demand. Only 4.5 per cent of elderly persons received home help, 0.79 per cent the services of a district nurse, 1.3 per cent meals on wheels and 7.30 per cent a chiropody service. It was found that 11.8 per cent of the elderly population received one or more of the domiciliary services and that a large percentage of these were in the 80-84 year age group. Townsend argued that the domiciliary services should compliment the services of the family and not replace them. The most important result of this survey was the guidelines produced for services based on observed and expressed needs of clients themselves. A 10 per cent increase in home help services was estimated as necessary to meet existing need, an over 5 per cent increase in mobile meals and an 11 per cent increase in chiropody services. Most elderly people surveyed received domiciliary services in the form of home help once or twice a week but this was a minimum service and did not meet demand. Estimates agreed that the increase necessary to meet demands would need to support an extra 600,000 elderly with home help, 350,000 with meals on wheels and 670,000 with the services of a chiropodist.[73] The Local Authority ten year plans did not show short fall in service, nor the need for increases in resources. They did however show all too clearly the large variations in levels of service between authorities. For example Rotherham provided 1.18 home helps per 1,000 of the elderly population over 65 and 0.30 nurses whereas Plymouth provided 0.08 home helps and 0.20 nurses per 1,000 of the elderly over 65 years. These figures could not be relied upon to give a true picture of the level of services as they did not in some cases take into account other services which supported the elderly such as Health Authority home helps.[74] The plans did not give the figures for hours of service provided or average number of hours service to clients.

On the information provided in the plans the Minister carried out a further review of 20 Local Authorities domiciliary services. As a result of this survey advice was given to authorities on the planning of services and charging policy. It was recognised that service to the elderly had expanded more than any other but that it still fell short of meeting the reasonable demands of the community. Services had been planned without the real extent of local need being known. Because of this lack of basic information Authorities were asked to undertake local studies to ascertain the need for services for the elderly.[75] Many Local Authorities lacked the will or expertise to undertake such research. This was recognised by the National Corporation for the Care of Old People who offered to carry out a national survey. This offer was accepted and a survey was carried out in 11 Local Authorities in Great Britian. The results published in 1968 showed all too clearly again the need for a large increase in services to the elderly both in content and extent and the need also to develop new methods of service delivery. As the 'Over 80s' survey in 1960 had shown this survey also pointed to a lack of public knowledge of services or how to get them.[76] The limited operation of domiciliary services at night and weekends had also caused concern since the early 1960s. Harris found that nearly 40 per cent of the mobile meals services provided by the WVS closed on holidays and that the service was very under provided. She called for an increase of 400 per cent to meet needs. This service had been pioneered by the WVS during the war and by 1978-1979 over 22 million meals were served to people living in their own homes. During the second world war the WVS attempted to provide food to the community through what were called communal factory canteens later renamed British Restaurants. The inadequate diet of the elderly caused Rowntree in 1947 to argue that the inadequate feeding of the elderly was due to war time conditions and that the continuation of war time meals service should be expanded to provide mobile meals such as existed in some areas of London. In 1947 about 6,000 meals were served and had risen to over one million in 1957. The meals on wheels scheme was such a success that the Government supported the development of this service in 1970.[77]

Because of the shortage of staff in the domiciliary services, and the hours worked, some home nurses and health visitors were undertaking tasks not requiring their professional skills which was taking up the amount of time they had to give to other clients. Despite widespread concern by welfare staff at the inadequate service and shortfall in domiciliary services attitudes of some staff hampered the development of the services. "There existed side by side with this concern, and sometimes in the same person, an authoritarian attitude towards old people which had led to the adoption of the view that welfare services were, for the elderly, a privilege, not a right".[78] This problem of attitudes towards the elderly and services for the elderly was to some extent responsible for the slow development of imaginative schemes to help them or involve them in helping themselves. Some Authorities however did examine their service to the elderly with a view to developing new schemes and extending others. Surrey County Council highlighted the large increase in services needed to offer a reasonable level of chiropody to the elderly. In 1976 90 per cent of persons helped by this service were aged 65 or over and in 1979 1,760,000 persons received this service. Over 90 per cent of Surrey's home help service in 1962 was to the elderly, because of the demand for the service they introduced a scheme of Neighbour Helps who looked after elderly persons. Huddersfield had in 1959 introduced a 24 hour, 7 day home help service because they did not feel that a service for 8 hours a day, 5 days a week really provided what they considered a reasonable standard of service. Any service offered outside normal hours was free.[79] Because of the different and diverse needs of the elderly full and part time staff were appointed to work evenings and weekends and some were allowed to arrange their own workload and hours of work. Harris put the need for a 41 per cent increase in the home help service alone in 1966 just to meet the needs of the elderly.

Some workers in the field were actually ignorant of such basic services for the elderly as home helps and meals on wheels and others had a lack of awareness of a need for a service at all. It was put forward that professionals did not always refer clients for services either because they did not know of the service or were unaware of the client's need.[80] Others argued that the service would have been managed better ty their profession. District nurses felt that under their direct management domiciliary services could have been used more effectively. The nurses response as reported by Hockey in 1966 showed a lack of understanding of the objectives of the domiciliary services. The report also outlined how they misused certain sections of the service such as home helps, whom they equated with the orderlies and domestics in hospital. Other professions far from not understanding the role of the domiciliary services actually were antagonistic towards them. Some General Practitioners felt that "they spend most of their time gossiping and drinking tea" and felt that some of the duties of the domiciliary staff should have been carried out by nurses. Many Doctors did not refer patients to the nursing services or domiciliary services because they thought the services overloaded and unable to cope with the extra work.[81] It was quite clear from these reports that the role of the nursing services and domiciliary services were not understood by those who should have known about the services. Interprofessional rivalry and jealousies were rampant, services were unco-ordinated and clients confused by the number of visitors from the 'welfare'. The services were in a disorganised state and this unnecessary deployment of professional staff was bound to have in the long run economic and professional consequences. This confusion was compounded by having 204 Health Authorities and the same number of Welfare Departments, some or all providing a range of domiciliary services for the elderly.

This state of affairs led to calls for change in the interests of the clients and economy.[82] As the use of social services and health services is diffused through the population over a far wider scale than ever before they have been used more and more by the middle classes who expose the services to more and more criticism and were ready to express judgement on the level and quality of service. A more knowledgeable and educated community meant a higher expectation of standards of care and a less unthinking acceptance of the traditional methods of service delivery. Community care or care in the community meant that more and more people were affected by the situation concerning the services. Care in the community allowed the elderly to keep their dignity and also their contact with friends. It did not matter whether the concept of care in the home had come about because of economic considerations or wishes to allow old people their dignity, the end result was the same, hopefully a happier, healthier elderly population. Community care also meant a new way of looking at and using existing services and viewing the service as a normal support in time of need rather than, as in the past, an interference or disruption in the life of the family. Others have seen the swing to community care as an arrogant imposition by social workers of their ideas about care of the elderly and families because of their emphasis on prevention. It has been stated that home support was justified by social workers in psychological rather than economic terms "views which are still widely held amongst social workers today, and the arrogance of the assumptions underlying such an approach still go unchallenged all too often".[83] Care in the community may have dangers for the elderly.

We must not think that the community is the only environment that an elderly person can have their needs met in. The only persons with a right to say which community care system is preferable are the elderly themselves. The concern of society at the waste of resources increased the impetus for some form of re-organisation to overcome these problems. The Government reacted by asking Lord Seebohm to "review the organisation of the responsibilities of Local Authority Personal Social Services in England and Wales".[84] As we shall see in the next chapter the recommendations of this committee led to the creation of a unified department to manage most of the personal social services in 1972. Would this new department lead to a more imaginative and creative use of domiciliary services? Would a department not managed by one of the recognised professions be powerful enough to argue for resources? Donnison in 1972 argued that "the creation of a service calls for considerable resources which can only be secured with the agreement of individual bodies outside the groups responsible for providing it".[85] Many had argued that the piecemeal development of domiciliary services was because it was for the most part under the control of the medical profession.

Summary

In this chapter I have explored some of what, I think, are the important influences that have helped shape the development of the domiciliary services for the elderly. It was not until this century that the elderly were recognised as a separate group in the community. Under the various Poor Laws, all those who suffered from poverty were dealt with in the same manner. The pensions legislation of 1908 and 1925 were some of the first attempts to help the elderly as a separate group with needs different from the rest of the disadvantaged groups in society.

The different services such as community nursing, home helps and meals on wheels did not originally begin as services for the elderly. The community nursing service was begun by William Rathbone whose experience in this field led him to set up the first district nursing service for the poor of Liverpool in 1859. By 1868 the East London Nursing Society had been formed along the lines of the Liverpool service. The Home Help Service had its origin in the Sick Room Help Society in the East End of London, which was used as a model for the domestic help service provided under the legislation in 1918 to help mothers and young children. Many of the difficulties suffered by working women and described in 'Maternity: Letters from Working Women' published by the Womens Co-operative Guild in 1915[86] were relieved to some extent by health services before the introduction of the welfare state in 1948. Services for the elderly were, however, very underdeveloped. The changing family structure, the increase in the numbers of the elderly, lack of domestic servants and the difficulties caused by the second world war, prompted the Government in 1944 to encourage Local Authorities to provide domestic home help support to the elderly. Reports in the late 1940's and 1950's however showed all too clearly that these services were falling far short of meeting the needs of the elderly in the community.

A perspective on the role of the family in supporting the elderly is necessary. The slow growth of domiciliary services reflected the concern that they would undermine the family. The family was seen at this period as the main support to the elderly. As shown by Sheldon in 1945, women were exploited.

Government attempts to draw up ten year plans in the 1960's highlighted the uneven distribution of services and differing standards in Authorities. Many bodies and Government reports at this time reported the problems caused by the lack of co-operation and co-ordination of services. These calls for co-operation which led to pressures for reorganisation of the social and health services are discussed in the next chapter.

Notes

1. Report of the enquiry into the cost of the National Health Service. Cmd. 9663, HMSO, 1956, p.12.

2. Royal Commission on the Poor Laws and Relief of Distress. Cd. 4499, HMSO, 1909.

3. B. Davis, Social Needs and Resources in Local Services (Michael Joseph, London, 1968).

4. L. Hockey, Care in the Balance (Queens Institute of District Nursing, London, 1968). M. Skeet, Home from Hospital (Macmillan Journals Ltd., London, 1974). M. Hardie and L. Hockey, Nursing Auxiliaries in Health Care (Croom Helm, London, 1978). C. Kratz, 'Bringing it Home', Nursing Times (26 October 1978).

5. Davis, Social Needs and Resources, p.27. W.D. Gynne, The Home Help Service in Cumbria (Social Service Department, Cumbria County Council, 1978). N. Howell, D. Boldy and B. Smith, Allocating the Home Help Service (Bedford Square Press, London, 1979).

6. Source: Jewish Board of Guardians, Annual Reports for 1886 to 1906 (Reports of the Ladies Conjoint Visiting Committee). See also Appendix No. XI (1), appendix to 3rd Vol., Evidence to the Royal Commission on the Poor Laws and The Relief of Distress. These sources give examples of a voluntary agencies efforts to provide domiciliary services in the form of home help and home nursing.

7. J.C. McVail, Report to the Royal Commission on the Poor Law and Relief of Distress, Appendix, Vol. XIV, Cd. 4499, HMSO, 1909.

8. Royal Commission on the Poor Laws and Relief of Distress, Minority Report, Ch. V. This chapter gives many examples of the effect of the lack of domiciliary care in the community; see also Ch. V Part B, Domiciliary Medical Treatment under the Poor Law.

9. Royal Commission on the Poor Laws and Relief of Distress, Appendix No. CXLVIII, para 6 to Vol. VIII; see also para 67 Vol. L Cd. 44990.

10. Royal Commission on the Poor Laws and Relief of Distress, Minutes of Evidence, Appendix IX, Vol. VI and VII, Q 72460, p.170. Mrs Hudson and Miss Walsh gave evidence of their experience of County Associations of Nursing. Their evidence is full of illuminating examples of the problems encountered by home nurses. See also the evidence of Mr Fleming, Q 9336 and Q 9337, p.424, Appendix Vol. 1,Cd. 4625 and

Appendix No. CXLVIII (para 6) to Vol VIII, Q 34672 and Q 75774.

11. Royal Commission on the Poor Laws and Relief of Distress, Part V, Ch. 2, para 169, page 360.

12. H. Frankel, 'The Industrial Distribution of the Population of Great Britain in July 1939', Journal of the Royal Statistical Society, Vol. CVIII, Parts III-IV (1945).

13. S. Ferguson and H. Fitzgerald, Studies in the Social Services (HMSO and Longmans, Green and Co., 1954). Chapter one outlines in some detail the effect upon the family of problems brought about by wartime conditions.

14. Report of The Womens Advisory Committee on The Domestic Service Problem, Ministry of Reconstruction, Cmd. 67, HMSO, 1919. This committee was established to 'Consider the general condition in regard to domestic service as effected by the employment of women on war work, and to indicate the general line on which the available supply of labour for this purpose may be utilised in the best interests of the Nation'. A sub-committee considered Home Helps, pp. 3-4.

15. Report of the Committee in Minimum Rates of Wages and Conditions of Employment in connection with Special Arrangements for Domestic Help. Ministry of Labour and National Service, Cmd. 6481, HMSO, 1943. See also Report on the Post-war Organisation of Private Domestic Employment, Ministry of Labour and National Service, Cmd. 6650, HMSO, 1945. This report recommended that the domiciliary home help service should be extended to the sick, infirm and elderly, paras 55-58.

16. In 1923 the Minister of Labour, Sir Montague Barlow, appointed a committee of women under the chairmanship of Mrs Ethel Wood to enquire 'into the present conditions as to the supply of female domestic servants'. Report of Committee on Domestic Service, Ministry of Labour, HMSO, London, 1923, para 53.

17. J.H. Sheldon, The Social Medicine of Old Age (Oxford University Press, London, 1948), p.46.

18. Ministry of Health, Circular 179/44: Domestic Help, 14 December 1944.

19. This number of over six and a half million accounts for the elderly over sixty-five, rather than men over 65 and women over 60.

20. Ministry of Health, Circular 179/44, 1944.

21. Ministry of Health, Circular 179/44, 1944.

22. L.M. Richey, 'The Home Help Service', Journal of the National Association of Home Help

Organisers (May, 1951), London.

23. Ministry of Health, Circular 51/49: Contributions to Old Peoples Welfare Organisations, 1949.

24. M. Bucke, 'Foster Care for the Elderly', Social Service Quarterly, Vol. XXX, No. 1, June/August. National Council for Social Services, London 1956. In Exeter and Plymouth elderly men and women were placed with households. Some of the elderly needed considerable care and support. Volunteers were trained to support the foster families.

25. Ministry of Health, Circular 11/59: Provision of Chiropody Services, 1959.

26. Ministry of Health, Circular 7/62: Co-operation with Voluntary Organisations, and Ministry of Health, Circular 18/62: Co-operation with Voluntary Organisations, 1962.

27. Ministry of Health, Circular 110/46: Home Helps and Domestic Helps, 1946.

28. Report on Private Domestic Employment. Cmd. 6650, 1945.

29. D.M. Elliott, 'The Status of Domestic Work in the United Kingdom', International Labour Review, Geneva, Vol. LXIII, No. 2 (Feb. 1951). See also Richey, 1951.

30. British Medical Association Report of a Committee to investigate the inadequate provision for the care and treatment of the elderly infirm 1946.

31. Old Age in a Modern World, Report of the third congress of the International Association of Gerontology, London, 1954 (E. and S. Livingstone Ltd., London, 1955).

32. B. Seebohm Rowntree, Old People (Oxford University Press, London, 1947). The date when Rowntree carried out this survey is not clear from the report.

33. Sheldon, Social Medicine.

34. Ministry of Health, Circular 118/47: Health Services to be provided under Part III of the National Health Services Act 1946, 1947.

35. WVS, Course for Organisers 1948, pp. 10-11.

36. N. Burr, The Home Help Service (Henry G. Morris, London, 1949). See also p.7.

37. H.D. Chalk and B. Benjamin, 'Eugeria: The contribution of the domestic help service', The Medical Officer (17 February 1951), pp. 65-67.

38. Report, Cost of the National Health Service, Cmd. 9663. See also p. 265 and paras 640-652, pp. 214-219.

39. Report of the Committee on the Economic and Financial Problems of the Provision for Old Age, Cmd. 9333, HMSO, 1954, para. 265. See also para. 647, Cmd. 9663, 1956.

40. Source: C.H. Wright and L. Roberts, 'The Place of the Home Help Service in the Care of the Aged', *The Lancet* (1 February 1958), p. 255.

41. Report Cost of the National Health Service, para. 15, p. 280.

42. Report on Co-operation between Hospital, Local Authority and General Practitioner Services, Central Health Services, HMSO, 1952.

43. See Wright and Roberts, 1958, Cmd. 9663, para. 617, 621. Lord Stonham House of Lords debate 13 December 1961, 337. Editorial *The Medical Cfficer* (12 August 1950). F. Brockington and S.M. Lempert, *The Social Needs of the Over 80s* (Manchester University Press, 1960).

44. Social Service in Action, Old Peoples Housework Scheme, *Social Services Quarterly*, Vol. XXVIII No. 3 (Dec. 1954/Feb. 1955), National Council for Social Services, 1954.

45. H.D. Chalk and B. Benjamin, *The Medical Officer*, (1951) see note 37.

46. Ministry of Health, Annual Report, Part 1, Cmd. 8342, 1951, p.48.

47. E.D. Irvine, 'The Place of the Health Department in the Care of the Aged', *The Medical Officer* (12 August 1950), pp.73, 75. Ministry of Health, Annual Report, 1954, Cmd. 2638, HMSO, 1955.

48. M. MacGregor and B. Benjamin, 'A Statistical Analysis of Home Nursing, London', *The Medical Officer* (25 November 1950), pp. 159-160.

49. A. Elliott, 'The Family Help and Night Attendant Services in Kent', *The Practitioner*, No. 1057, Vol. 177 (July 1956), pp. 38-47.

50. L. Nepean-Gubbins,'The Contribution of the Home Help Organiser to the Welfare of the Aged', *RSH Journal*, No. 2, Vol. 78 (Nov-Dec. 1958).

51. A.D. Symons, 'The Welfare of Old People', *The Medical Officer* (7 October 1950), p. 158.

52. Ministry of Health, Circular 11/50: Welfare of Old People, 1950.

53. The Home Help Service, *The Medical Officer* (22 April 1950), p. 157.

54. G. Gordon, J.G. Thompson and A.R. Emerson, 'Domiciliary Services for the Over Sixties', *The Medical Officer* (12 July 1957), pp. 19-24.

55. Lord Amulree, 'The Care of Old People at Home', *The Practitioner*, No. 1057, Vol. 177

(July 1956), p. 33-37.

56. Ministry of Health, Annual Report 1953, Part II, Cmd. 9307, p. 194. See also Elliott, The Practitioner (July 1956), p.42.

57. Over Seventy, National Council of Social Services, July 1954, Table 26, p.35. Old People in Sheffield (Sheffield Council of Social Service, 1949). Sheldon, Social Medicine of Old Age, 1948.

58. Ministry of Health, Circular 11/50: Welfare of Old People, 1950.

59. Over Seventy, p.30 and J.H. Sheldon, 'The Role of the Aged in the Modern Society', BMJ (11 February 1950).

60. G. Sumner and R. Smith, Planning Local Authority Services for the Elderly (George Allen and Unwin, London, 1969), p.33. Medical Officer of Health, Annual Report 1955, Rotherham 1956, p.79 and Ministry of Health, Annual Report 1961, Cmd. 1754, 1962, p.87.

61. 'Kylie News' (July 1982), No. 3, London, p.1.

62. Ministry of Health, Circular 14/57, para.15, 1957.

63. Brockington and Lempert, The Social Needs of the Over 80s, p.51.

64. Report of the Committee on Local Authority and Allied Personal Social Services, Cmd. 3703, HMSO, 1969, Appendix F.

65. Brockington and Lempert, The Social Needs of the Over 80s, p.51 and p.80.

66. Lord Newton, H.L. Debate 403, 1961.

67. P. Townsend, 'The Timid and the Bold', New Society, No. 34 (23 May 1963), pp.16-18.

68. National Health Service Hospital Plan for England and Wales. Ministry of Health, Cmd. 1604, HMSO, 1962, para.31.

69. R. Klien and J. Ashley, 'Old-age Health', New Society, No. 484 (6 January 1972), p.14.

70. Source: J. Hanson, 'Challenge to the Welfare Services', Municipal Review, Vol. 36, No. 431. (November 1965), p.666. See also correspondence in New Society, No. 36 (6 June 1963), p.29.

71. Sumner and Smith, Services for the Elderly, pp.208-209.

72. Sumner and Smith, Services for the Elderly, p.210.

73. P. Townsend, The Family Life of Old People (Penguin Books Ltd, London, 1957). See also Table 2 p. 24.

74. Health and Welfare, Cmd. 1973, HMSO, 1963.

75. Ministry of Health, Circular 26/65: Home Help Service, 1965.

76. A.I. Harris, *Social Welfare for the Elderly* (HMSO, London, 1968).

77. DHSS Circular 5/70, 1970.

78. S. Sainsbury, E. Blackaby and M. Savage. 'A Pilot Survey into Domiciliary Welfare Services for older people in the Borough of Fulham', unpublished, London School of Economics, 1963, pp.24 and 46.

79. Report of the Working Party on Welfare Services for Old People in Surrey, Surrey County Council, London 1962; see p.9. R.G. Davis, 'Towards a fuller Home Help Service', *The Journal of The Institute of Home Help Organisers*, Vol. 9, No. 17 (1961), pp.15-17.

80. A.F. McCourbrey and I.A.G. MacQueen, 'A Survey of Old People in a Rural Community', *Health Bulletin*, Vol. X, No. 3, 1952. A.I. Harris, *Social Welfare for the Elderly*, p. 65.

81. L. Hockey, *Care in the Balance*, pp.83, 183 and 126.

82. See: Cmd. 2742, 1965, Cmd. 9663, 1966, Cmd. 169, 1959. *Half our Future*, HMSO, 1963, Cmd. 9333, 1954.

83. E. Wilson, *Women and the Welfare State* (Tavistock, London, 1977), p.88.

84. Committee: Personal Social Services, Cmd. 3703, para.l.

85. D.V. Donnison, *Social Policy and Administration Revisited* (George Allen and Unwin, London, 1975), revised ed., p.101.

86. M. Llewlyn Davis (ed.), *Maternity: Letters from Working Women* (G. Bell and Sons Ltd., London, 1915).

Chapter Two

THE SEEBOHM ERA - A STEP IN THE DARK

The diversity of the domiciliary care service for the elderly can only be understood when seen against the struggle by the various groups that make up the present day service which emerged from the domination of the medical, nursing and social work professions. Also the events surrounding the political decision by the Labour Government in 1969 to place the domiciliary services in the then new proposed Social Service Department in Local Government Authorities must be taken into account. The changing age structure of society has also to be considered against the policy of community care for the elderly in their home instead of hospitals and other institutions. The piecemeal development and organisation of the present service must be viewed against this political and economic social background.

A constant theme running through the history and development of the domiciliary services since the beginning of the twentieth century is the conflict between workers in the domiciliary care service and nursing and social work professions and the ensuing role confusion. Some of this confusion is due to the essential central caring nature of the different professions but by far most is caused, because of the parallel development of the services without any co-ordination or co-operation by those planning the different services. Each professional group has tried to meet the needs of the elderly clients as seen by them without taking into account the work of other agencies. The subordinate position and role of the domiciliary services to nursing, medicine and social work has meant that the full potential of the service has not been realised because of either the lack of interest or expertise on the part of these professions, or their wish to dominate the service and place it in a subservient role to their own profession. The domiciliary services have not been allowed to take their rightful place as one of the services which is central and vital to the care of the elderly and in the forefront of the fight against the problems of old age. The domiciliary services are now by and far the largest single spenders in many social service departments.

The beginning of this conflict between the different professions can be traced to the beginning of the 20th century. The uneconomic use of qualified nurses was recognised in 1911 by Dr McVail when he put forward the view that there was a need for someone other than qualified nursing staff to help old people in the community by washing and bathing them, providing a laundry service and keeping the house clean.

He was arguing in 1909 for the setting up of the equivalent of today's home help and auxillary community nursing service. Others who gave evidence to the committee supported his view that qualified nurses were not used effectively and they called for more supportive domiciliary services.[1]

Local Authorities were not empowered to provide domiciliary services for the elderly until 1944 so the District Nursing Service was the only domiciliary support the elderly received in the community apart from a restricted meals on wheels service provided by voluntary agencies. The shortage of qualified nurses and the cost of training them forced nursing organisations to find other ways of providing more efficient and cheaper services. Cottage Nurses were recruited. These nurses worked under the supervision of qualified nurses and lived in the homes of their patients. "They did not do trained nursing work, but they do the general work of getting the patient in a condition to benefit by trained nursing ... that is they clean the cottage, they are willing to live in the cottage, they will do the cooking, they will keep the windows open, they will take the sack of straw out of the chimney and clear out the accumulation from under the bed, they will wash the people and see that the beds are properly made and properly sheeted and that patients are dressed, properly washed and kept clean".[2] The domiciliary worker in the community at the beginning of the century was either an untrained nurse such as a cottage nurse or a person employed to do domestic tasks in the homes of families with a sick member or needing help and support with a small baby.

By 1920 the blurring of roles of the home helps and nursing personnel was causing concern at the highest level in the new Ministry of Health. In the first report of the Chief Medical Officer of the Ministry of Health attention was drawn to the fact that the home help service was not a nursing service and that home help staff should never carry out nursing duties.[3] The Chief Medical Officer was emphatic that the domiciliary service was a purely domestic service. This definition of the domestic supportive role of the domiciliary service was further emphasised by the medical profession in 1920 and again in 1937.[4]

In 1928 the Liverpool Personal Social Service Society was one of the first voluntary services to set up a committee whose primary aim was the care of the elderly in the community and poor law institutions.[5] By 1940 the number of unco-ordinated efforts by agencies to help the elderly was causing concern at national level. This concern led the National Council of Social Services to call together under the Chairmanship of Miss Eleanor Rathbone MP a national committee to organise and encourage local committees for the care of the aged to co-ordinate services at a local level. Co-ordination at local level after 1940 was through Old Peoples Welfare or Care Committees upon which sat representatives of statutory and voluntary agencies involved with providing services for the elderly in the community. This attempt at rationalising the services to the elderly was a failure. The creation of the National Health Service in 1948 tried to resolve this problem but did not. "The need for co-ordination in the health service was emphasised but not created by the National Health Service".[6] The creation of the National Health Service complicated the already chaotic situation by creating a tripartite structure, the Hospital Service, the General Practitioner Service and Local Authority Health and Welfare Services all which cut across central government departmental boundaries and client groups. The Committee on the Economic and Financial Problems of the Provision for Old Age in 1954 expressed concern at the amount of unco-ordinated visiting to the elderly in the community caused by this divided responsibility. By 1956 voices in the medical profession argued for one Local Authority Committee to manage health and welfare services for the elderly. The division between the services offered by hospitals and local authorities was however, considered a more serious divide in the National Health Service.

Attempts by various Health Departments to close this divide by developing domiciliary care teams to care for the elderly in the community under the leadership of General Practitioners was praised in some quarters. There was however very little enthusiasm in 1956 to create new systems to improve co-operation in services for the elderly.[7] Inter service rivalries caused delays in co-ordinating services and hindered the development of more appropriate and effective services for the elderly.[8] By 1968 there were 129 local authority welfare committees, 28 health committees and 18 authorities which provided services through a combined health and welfare committee.[9]

The growth in Health and Welfare public expenditure between 1952 and 1968 had risen over 152 per cent. Health expenditure had risen from 1,100 million pounds to 2,142 million in 1968. Welfare expenditure had risen from 35 million pounds to 117 million pounds. A rise of 234 per cent over 16 years.

This confused situation, the rapid expansion and growth of welfare services and the increasing cost of providing these services, all contributed to the call for change and a more efficient and co-ordinated service.

The switch from institutional care to care in the community of the elderly and mentally ill in the 1960's meant that local authorities had to think seriously about the quality and type of care that was appropriate and of the problems of finding the right calibre of staff to implement their policies.

Community Care at this time was not simply involving professional workers in the community, it also required the community to be vigilant and tolerant of social casualties living in their midst and to play their part in the care of those persons. As the policy of community care gained public and professional acceptance, the policy increased the demand for more social workers, home helps, home nurses and other domiciliary staff. The development of a community care policy highlighted the difficulty of getting the disparate professions to co-operate in a team effort to support clients in the community. This lack of co-operation was caused partly by administrative problems but it also reflected different professional attitudes. The distrust and lack of professional co-operation was particularly evident in the provision of service for the elderly. Any or all of the agencies or individuals in Diagram 2.1 could have been involved

Diagram 2.1 Agencies involved in providing Health and Welfare Services to Elderly in Community pre 1971

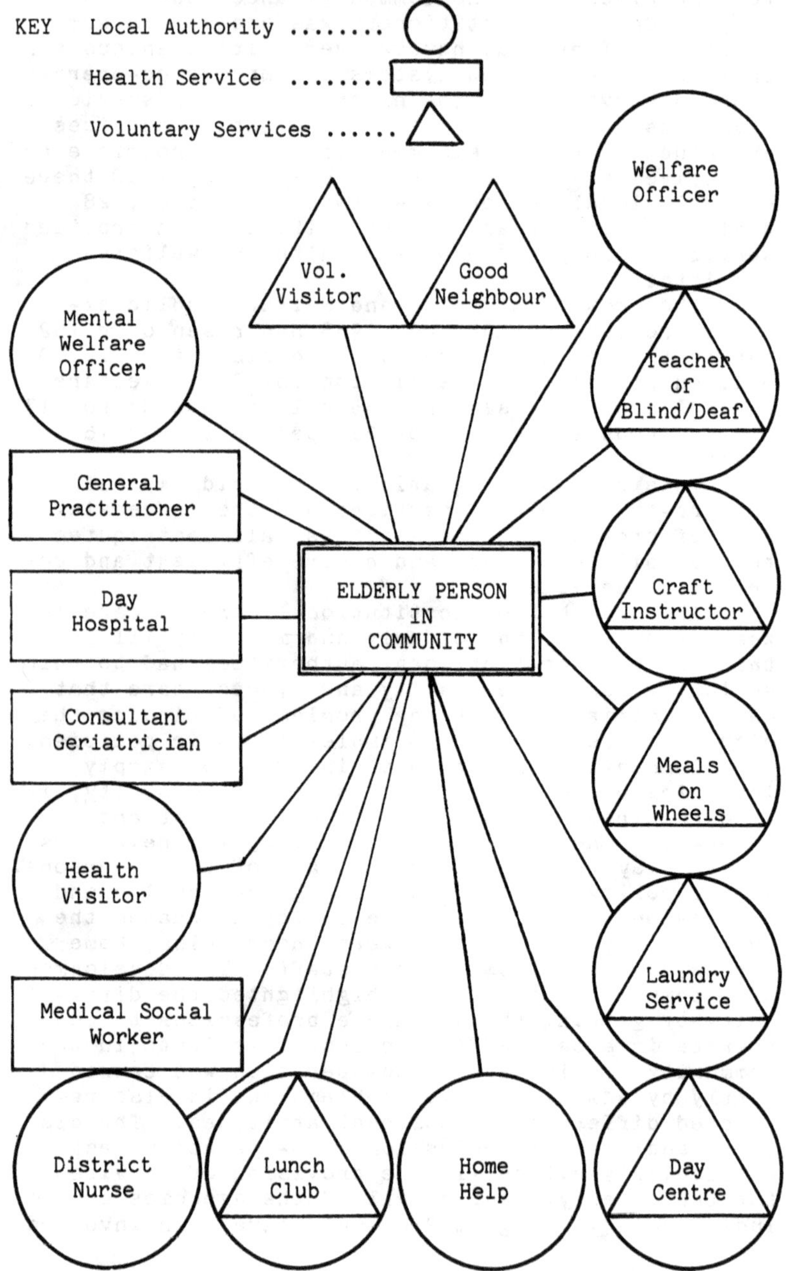

in providing a service to an elderly person living in the community at any one time. No person or agency was the leader or co-ordinator of the services, each worker or agency was responsible for his own specialist contribution. The result was a fragmented and ineffective service. One particular inquiry carried out in 1971 investigated the organisational structure of the Health Service by observation of the users and evaluated the degree of co-ordination and co-operation between the various services. Twenty seven per cent of the cases examined showed positive failure in the provision of services. The research highlighted many examples of lack of co-operation between agencies and individuals and inadequate services. The domiciliary care services it was found filled many of the gaps not covered by other services.[10]

Social workers had always worked in specialist areas such as mental health, child care or work with the elderly. This specialisation was condemned by the Jameson Report in 1956[11] because it caused overlapping and complicated family visiting. The Younghusband report on social workers in health and welfare departments in 1959 went much further and advocated a family social worker who would not specialise in any particular area of work[12] but would work with the whole family. The first call for a family social service was put forward by a committee set up by the Labour party in 1964. This committee also reported that the "administrative structure of the social service is ripe for review so that they may grow and develop coherently to meet the need of an increasingly complex society". A later report also called for a family social service.[13] Because of increasing pressures for change a committee was asked to review the organisation and responsibilities of Local Authority Personal Social Services in 1965 (Seebohm Committee). Despite the importance of this inquiry the committee made no attempt to commission independent research in the area it was to review and made recommendations, which changed the face of the personal social services for many years. Shortages in the amount of services, inadequate and poor quality services were highlighted. The report concluded that the main reasons for these problems was lack of resources caused by the small size of agencies, divided responsibilities across these agencies and a lack of research on which methods of work could be evaluated.

The Seebohm Committee reported in 1969 and one of its recommendations was for the setting up of a new Local Authority Department. This department would manage the services for children, the welfare services and some of the social services provided by Health Departments such as home helps and mental health services.

The reactions of the various professional groups to the recommendations of this committee are well documented in Halls book 'Reforming the Welfare'.[15] In this chapter I shall only be concerned with the reactions of the various groups concerned with services for the elderly and of the effects of their activities upon the development of domiciliary services.

The British Medical Association in their evidence to the Seebohm Committee argued for a combined health and social services department under the management of the Medical Officer of Health. Some Local Authorities had already organised their social welfare and health services in this manner and were criticised in parliament for so doing.[16] There was growing pressure from social work groups for the implementation of the committee recommendations, the setting up of a Social Service Department under the leadership of a Director of Social Services. This organised pressure for change "puzzled" the medical profession and they regretted "the belligerent pressure for immediate implementation of the Seebohm proposals" a strange attitude to adopt by the medical profession on pressure groups in view of their actions during the negotiations leading up to the creation of the National Health Service in the 1940's. They argued that this pressure was not in the best interests of the new service.[17]

Those who were responsible for the management of domiciliary services for the elderly on the whole wished not to join the new Social Services Department but to stay under the direction of the Medical Officer. In 1966 the Institute of Home Help Organisers who were responsible for organising the largest section of the domiciliary services for the elderly wrote to the British Medical Association, The Society of Medical Officers of Health and the Queens Institute of District Nursing expressing their deep concern at any attempt to remove them from the "present position of anciliary to the Medical Officer of Health and Domiciliary Nursing Service". The Institute put forward the view that its service existed to further the work of the General Practitioner, Health Visitor and District Nurse and so they canvassed support from these Organisations for the view that they, the Home Help Service, should remain in the Health Service.[18]

The Institute was so concerned at having to work closer with social workers that they requested an opportunity from the Seebohm Committee to press home their views by giving oral evidence to support their written submission. The Queens Institute of District Nursing, Royal College of Nursing, the Royal College of Midwives, the Health Visitors Association and the Society of Medical Officers of Health offered support to the Institute and indicated that their organisations' evidence to the committee did not conflict in any way with the view that the Institute had of the role of the Home Help Service.[19] Later in 1971 the Royal College of Nursing was putting forward a policy that Health Authorities should set up their own home help service.[20]

The Home Help Organisers hoped that, by stating the importance of medical personnel in the assessment of clients needs for the Home Help Service, the committee would recommend that they stay in the Health Department. In the Institute of Home Help Organisers written evidence to the Committee they stated that the assessment of need should be based on medical recommendation only and that the level of demand should be controlled by medical recommendation. Members of the Institute met the Committee on the 6th January 1967 to support these views in person. They orally supported their written evidence by stating that the service was a fundamental part of the medical and nursing team. The prospect of working in a department headed by a social worker "horrified" them. The home help staff saw themselves as practical people who found it difficult to work with social workers. They saw the service developing more towards the support of nursing services rather than that of social work and for that reason needed the advice of medical officers to help them set priorities.[21]

How strongly the Institute felt about social worker control can be evidenced by the manner in which they dealt with a request from social workers for copies of their written evidence to the committee. The Institute had made available to universities and institutions copies of their evidence but refused a copy of this non confidential information to a Childrens Officer who had requested it. They felt that of all heads of social services a Childrens Officer was the one least likely to be directly interested in the home help service.[22] This attitude, which could be seen as a fear of social workers, continues in the policy of the Institute of Home Help Organisers today.[23] The Institute contemplated some form of action by their members if they were forced to transfer to the new Department but did not carry this threat out. The Seebohm Committee considered the arguments in favour of the Domiciliary services being a medical service. As most of the clients in a new unified social service department would be potential clients of the domiciliary services, social criteria were important in the assessment for a home help service and therefore the committee put forward that the domiciliary service should become part of the new Department.[24] After the publication of the Report in 1968 the Institute reassessed its position and wrote to the Minister of Health agreeing that the Home Help Service would work just as well in the new proposed department as in the old Health Department although not all domiciliary organisers agreed.[25] Many expressed mixed feelings that the new Chief Officer of the Social Services Department might not be able to command resources for the service as did the Medical Officer of Health.[26] These professional rivalries had played a part in preventing the full development of the service up to 1971. At the time of the coming into operation of the Social Service Departments the Home Help Service was the only comprehensive domiciliary service available to the elderly. Other services such as chiropody, meals on wheels, laundry or neighbour helps were very disorganised and the quality and quantity of the services varied from authority to authority.

Very few elderly persons used the domiciliary nursing and home help services in 1971. Only about 3 per cent used the district nurse, 5 per cent the home help, 2 per cent the chiropody service and 1.6 per cent the meals on wheels service. In 1970 some 10,000 people in their own homes received over 13,000,000 meals.[27] There was a striking variation in both the standard and rates of provision between Local Authorities. The average rate of provision was 56.6 meals per thousand elderly in Great Britain. In London the rate varied from 27.8 to 231.6 per thousand of the elderly in the Local Boroughs. The criteria of assessment for meals was difficult to determine but generally meals were offered to those elderly who were housebound, lived alone and could not obtain a hot nutritious meal except by the receipt of the meals on wheels service. The function of the service was viewed as a vital support service providing meals of nutritive value as to make a significant contribution to the food intake of the elderly person.

Many of those who received the service lived alone and were isolated. Many lived near shops but very few did their own shopping. This inability to shop was placed on the feebleness of the elderly receiving the service,[28] but later research has shown that many home helps can make clients over dependent on domiciliary services which may account for this fact.[29] Over 35 per cent of those receiving the meals service had their shopping carried out by home helps.

The Meals on Wheels service delivered meals to most clients five days a week. Many elderly people who did not receive the service at weekends did not wish the meals on Saturday and Sunday because they feared the loss of visits by relatives or friends. Many more preferred to cook their own meals, however some old people were prepared to go without meals on weekends rather than request a seven day service. On the days that no meal was provided there was a considerable drop in the nutritive value of the meals eaten even though most ate a cooked meal. Many old people only ate snacks on days no meal was delivered others ate very little or part of a meal delivered on the day before. Most of the meals eaten at weekends were prepared by the elderly persons themselves and there was a dependence on convenience foods.

None of those elderly persons receiving the service felt that they should never be reassessed for their suitability to receive the service but most believed that they should themselves decide if they wished to be removed from the receipt of meals.[30]

In 1971 the powers of Local Authorities to provide social services for the elderly were limited to the provision of home help, meals on wheels, residential accommodation and the provision of support to voluntary organisations to provide services. All these powers were continued under the Health Service and Public Health Act 1968 which allowed authorities to widen the availability of such services as housing, chiropody and domiciliary services to a larger client group. The main aim of the 1968 Act was to provide a preventative service "and thus to promote the welfare of the elderly generally and so far as possible prevent or postpone personal or social deterioration or breakdown". Authorities were not directed to provide a certain standard of services but the Minister allowed and encouraged experimentation.

Section 45 had been delayed in implementation because of the economic situation, but even in 1972 the Secretary of State for Social Services expected that the new services would be restricted because of financial limitations even though he had given Local Authorities additional capital for services for the elderly.[31] Under these new powers Local Authorities were able to rationalise their domiciliary services and either redeploy staff or employ new staff to co-ordinate services for the elderly.[32] Some Authorities placed Domiciliary Services Organisers as managers of combined home help, laundry services and meals on wheels services. Social workers organised boarding out schemes for the elderly and the provision of aids and adaptations in clients own homes.

Before setting up new services local authorities were requested to research the needs of the elderly and to plan services in close co-operation with Health Services and Voluntary Organisations.

The special needs of the over 75's was recognised and put forward as a priority. The home help service was given the highest priority as was the development of Voluntary Visiting of the Elderly and the development of social centres to provide meals and meals on wheels services.[33]

Section 45 of the Health Service and Public Health Act 1968 came into force on the 1st April 1972. The decision by the Government to implement this section of the Act at this time was reached in the light of the development of the new Social Service Departments and the task imposed upon them by the Chronically Sick and Disabled Persons Act 1970. It was hoped that the Social Service Department would use the powers invested by Section 45 in reorganising their social work and health services.

The provision of a Home Help Service became a central government priority. Section 13 of the Health Services and Public Health Act 1968 replaced the permissive power of the Local Authority to provide a home help service if they wished with a duty to provide such a service adequate to the needs of their areas. The power to provide laundry services for the elderly was also widened. The Government recognised that the majority of clients supported by the home help and domiciliary services were the elderly and argued for the Authorities to provide the service not to individuals but to households. This change in policy was a great help and provided practical assistance to relatives caring for the elderly. The Ministry called for an increase in the domiciliary services provided. In looking at the home help service organisation it was argued that it must form part of a balanced and co-ordinated domiciliary team with good links with the health services. The social and caring rather than the purely domestic nature of the service was re-enforced which confirmed the recommendation of the Seebohm Committee to place the service in Social Service rather than the Medical Department.[34]

Summary

I have outlined the confusion which runs through the development of the domiciliary services for the elderly caused by the lack of central Government leadership or planing since 1944. The difficulties caused by this lack of planing and co-ordination led to pressure on Government to set up a Committee to examine the issues, which in turn led to the recommendation of that committee to set up a new department to manage all of the personal social services. A constant theme which has emerged in this chapter is the role confusion between the various caring professions and the resulting conflict. The first attempts by Government to try and co-ordinate the services of the different groups and agencies helping the elderly were discussed and the attempts by the medical profession to head any new initiatives.

The Seebohm Committee, which recommended the bringing together of all the groups of workers who provided personal social services, was discussed and the Committee's relationship with the professional organisation that represented Domiciliary Organisers in the new department was analysed. The Government's decision to implement Section 45 of the Health Services and Public Health Act 1968 in 1972 was examined. This Act reflected Government's concern at this time to give priority to services for the elderly and placed a mandatory responsibility upon Local Authorities to provide domiciliary services. How this decision affected services for the elderly and resource allocation in both the Health and Local Authority fields are discussed in the next chapter.

Notes

1. J. C. McVail, Report of the Royal Commission on the Poor Law and Relief of Distress, Appendix Vol., Cd. 4499,HMSO,1909. See also Q75774 and Q72458.

2. Royal Commission on the Poor Laws and the

Relief of Distress. Cd. 4625, Q9337, HMSO, 1909.

3. Ministry of Health, First Annual Report. Cd. 923, HMSO, 1920.

4. Ministry of Health, 1st Report of the Welsh Consultative Council on Medical and Allied Services. Cd. 703, HMSO, 1920. Ministry of Health, Report of an Investigation into Maternal Mortality. Cd. 5422, HMSO, 1937.

5. N. Roberts, *Our Future Selves* (George Allen and Unwin, London, 1970), p.27.

6. See page 235, Cd. 9663, Report of the Committee of Enquiry into the Cost of the National Health Service, HMSO, 1956, and Central Health Services Council Report on Co-operation between Hospital, Local Authority and General Practitioner Services, HMSO, 1952, paras. 9 and 10.

7. Report of the Committee on the Economic and Financial Problems of the Provision for Old Age. Cd. 9333, HMSO, 1954, para. 266. See also paras 606, 616 and 710 Cd. 9663, 1956.

8. Report of the Committee on Children and Young Persons. Cd. 1191, HMSO, 1960.

9. Report of the Committee on Local Authority and Allied Personal Social Services. Cd. 3703, HMSO, 1968.

10. B. Scammells, *The Administration of Health and Welfare Services* (Manchester University Press, 1971), pp.90-104.

11. Report of the Committee on Health Visiting, HMSO, 1956.

12. Report of the Committee on Social Workers in the Local Authority Health and Welfare Services, HMSO, 1959.

13. Crime: A Challenge to us All. Report of a Labour Party Study Group (June 1964). See also Children and Young Persons in Scotland. Cd. 2306, HMSO, 1964.

14. Cd. 3703, HMSO, 1968.

15. P. Hall, *Reforming the Welfare* (Heinemann Educational Books, London, 1976).

16. See: *The Medical Officer* (9 August 1968), p.90 (30 May 1969), p.301; A.D.C.S. Cameron, 'Administration of a Local Authority Community Services', *Public Service*, Vol. CXXI (September 1968).

17. 'Seebohm Sophistry and Green Paper Gallimaufry', *The Medical Officer*, Vol. CXXI (18 April 1969), pp.207-208.

18. Letters to the Society of Medical Officers of Health, The Royal College of Nursing, Royal

College of Midwives, Health Visitors Association and The Queens Institute of District Nursing (Institute of Home Help Organisers, Archives, London).

19. Archives of The Institute of Home Help Organisers, London.

20. D.J. Parker and S.S. Fish, 'Help for the Home Help Service', _British Hospital and Social Service Review_ (25 Sept. 1971), pp. 1981-1983.

21. Archive of The Institute of Home Help Organisers, 1966-1972. See also paras. 376-377 of Cd. 3703, HMSO, 1968.

22. Internal Memorandum. Archives of The Institute of Home Help Organisers, dated 23 April 1968.

23. 'Evidence to the Enquiry into the Role of Social Workers', _The Newsletter_, The Institute of Home Help Organisers (August 1981), p.8.

24. Cd. 3703, HMSO, 1968 para. 377.

25. Letter to the Minister of Health, 19 November 1968, Archives of The Institute of Home Help Organisers, London.

26. D. Carter, 'The Home Help Service in Social Service Departments - Problems and Opportunities', _The Journal of The Institute of Home Help Organisers,_ Vol. 19, No. 55 (December 1971), London, pp.7-9.

27. DHSS Circular 5/70: Organisation of Meals on Wheels, 1970.

28. B.R. Stanton, Meals for the Elderly (King Edwards Hospital Fund, London, 1971).

29. N.A. Malin, 'Group Homes for Mentally Handicapped Adults'. Unpublished PhD. Thesis, University of Sheffield, 1980.

30. B. Stanton, _Meals for the Elderly_ (King Edwards Hospital Fund, London, 1971) see Table 6, and also pp.47 and 51.

31. DHSS Circular 19/71: Welfare of the Elderly March 1971.

32. DHSS, _Review of the Home Help Service in England_ (Social Work Service, 1973).

33. DHSS Circular 19/71, 1971.

34. DHSS Circular 53/71: Help in the Home, October 1971.

Chapter Three

DEVELOPMENTS IN THE 1970s

The development of Domiciliary Services for the elderly across the country is of course a continuing process. To obtain a true picture of the totality of the service is, therefore, difficult. Local and voluntary agencies were in different stages of development and many did not publish statistics or reports of their work. An overall view of the service could therefore, only be extricated from those statistics which were available and from the few studies which have been reported. Several factors must be taken into account in discussing Domiciliary Services for the elderly. Philosophies of care change over time, better standards of care and living conditions are expected as is a better quality of life, the structure of the family is changing, the elderly person's needs are changing as the population structure changes and more and more elderly persons over eighty-five survive. All these factors are interlinked and at different points in time some are more important than others. Many pronouncements have been made by various Governments in the past few years on the elderly. These observations, the last of which were outlined in 'Growing Older' in 1982 have been the first attempts, although feeble, to review the place and role of old people in society and the services needed to support them to live in their own homes. These attempts to influence policy and planning have had a number of important themes running through them. All the papers have continued the preference for Domiciliary Services and community based care. Also more and more emphasis has been placed on efforts to support those who look after their elderly relatives or friends or neighbours and the place of voluntary agencies in providing community services.[1]

The turn to the concept of community care or

care in the community which began in the early 1960s and developed in the 1970s, was strongly reiterated in 1976 in 'Priorities for the Health and Personal Services' and continued in nearly all subsequent guidance to local authorities and health authorities. Very few of these reports pointed out that community care was not necessarily cheaper than residential care.[2] Many of the guidelines or norms set for services for the elderly were formulated in the 1960s and early 1970s and Social Service plans were drawn up in 1972. However, since the plans were published the setback in the economy and expenditure policy on spending in the public sector have cast doubt on the continued validity of these guidelines and targets today.

'Care in Action' in 1981 finally brought home the problem of expenditure cuts "as the growth in financial resources are severely limited and the priority groups are large, further progress cannot be rapid and will depend mainly on skilful use of innovative approaches including the greater use of what the voluntary and private sector can contribute".[3] In chapter 5 some of the attempts of local authorities to meet this challenge are discussed. The report 'Growing Older' places importance on statutory support for groups and individuals who provide direct support to the elderly. "The Government sees the primary role of the public services as an enabling one, helping people to care for themselves and their families by providing a framework of support".[4] Domiciliary Services, therefore, in the 1970s and 1980s, because of these policies became the subject of numerous pressures to be effective and efficient. The service had become aware of the need to support relatives and neighbours who play a positive role in the care of the elderly. Also elderly people were more and more being allowed and encouraged to make choices about the nature and amount of help they needed. Because of the pressures on resources, assessment methods have been the object of examination and concern, to ensure the most effective use of both manpower and financial resources. Many have also become concerned about the overlap of responsibility of services for the elderly between the provision made by the Health and Social Services. Since the re-organisation of the personal social services in 1971 the domiciliary services have grown despite severe economic restraints of Local Government spending. From 1971 to 1979 there was a 15 per cent increase in the number of Organisers. From 1,058 in 1971 to 1,377 in 1979.

There was a 64 per cent increase in home helps with only a 6.7 per cent in the number of clients. In 1972, 289 organisers supervised 6,222 home helps who visited 92,729 cases, by 1979 there was 180 organisers, a drop of 39, supervising 5,956 home helps giving a service to 59,000 clients.[5] The rate of clients to home helps was 14:1 in 1971 and this had fallen to 8:1 in 1979. This was nearly an 80 per cent increase in the provision of home helps in ratio to the number of clients but in London as a whole for example, there was a considerable drop in the number of both home help staff and organisers from 1974, with a corresponding drop in the number of clients served. By and far the largest client group helped by the Domiciliary Services were the over sixty fives. By 1974 84.3 per cent of cases in Greater London were clients over sixty five years of age and in England in 1976 this had risen to 87.9 per cent.

In England and Wales the number of elderly persons visited by the service rose from 249,000 in 1961 to 396,000 in 1970 and to 704,000 in 1980. There was a corresponding drop in visits to the elderly by the home nursing service, 231,000 visits in 1961 to 168,000 in 1976. The provision of meals on wheels increased from 140,000 meals in 1971 to 194,000 meals in 1976.[6] It would seem that the cut back and decrease in the home nursing service was compensated for and met somewhat by an increase in the domiciliary services.

The change from Health Department administration to Social Services Department management in 1971 brought with it very little disturbance to the domiciliary services or a reduction in the quality of service to clients. Sixty four Local Authorities attempted to integrate their domiciliary services into the new social service area teams. These teams were made up of social service staff providing a number of social services serving a small section of the Local Authority area. Many Domiciliary Service Organisers found that they were quickly accepted as full members of the social services team.[7]

Directors of Social Services proved keen to develop the services from a purely domestic one to one with a strong caring function. Widespread dissatisfaction, with the tripartite structure of the National Health Service especially within the medical profession led to the call for a reorganisation of the Health Services. The election of a Conservative government in 1970 which was committed to improving the efficiency of the management of Central and Local Government meant more central government involvement in local planning. This need for central guidance was made even more important with the reorganisation of the Health Services and Local Government in 1974. Both the Labour and Conservative parties were in principal agreed that a unified Health and Local Authority service would be ideal as there was a great deal of substitution between the services, particularly for the elderly. However because of pressure from the Medical and Local Government lobbies this did not happen. The social work and welfare aspects of the Health Services were transfered to the Local Authority and the health services managed by Local Authorities were placed under Health Services control. The Domiciliary Nursing services were also transfered from Local Authority to Health Services.

The National Health Service Reorganisation Act 1973 required the setting up of Joint Consultative Committees to help co-ordinate health and social services planning at local level. Advice was given by Central Government as to the composition and method of working of these co-ordinating committees.[8] This attempt to overcome planning difficulties however did nothing to overcome the wide variations in standards and quality of services between authorities. Barbara Castle the Secretary of State for Social Services in 1976 in a forward to the Consultative document 'Priorities for the Health and Personal Social Services in England' emphasised that central government must set national guidelines. The publication of this consultative document was a new departure in government policy, it was an attempt to establish rational and systematic priorities for the health and social services. This need to set priorities was made all the more urgent by the Labour government's economic policies which had led to restrictions on public expenditure. Local Government in particular was hit by these restrictions. The rapid growth in public expenditure and in particular in the personal social services which had been rising at a rate of 14 per cent per year had stopped. Any growth in services had to be financed by corresponding savings or economies in other areas.

In order to encourage and help Health and Local Authorities to plan and provide services for priority groups, special finance (called Joint Finance) was made available to Joint Care Planning Teams, which had been set up by Joint Consultative Committees to plan services which fell into government categories of priority. Services for the elderly formed a priority and it was felt imperative that the right balance in both Health and Social Service be achieved. 'Joint Financing' however was discretionary and many local authorities did not take advantage of the opportunity.[9]

The government's aim of setting priorities was to restate the importance of the role of primary care in the community to relieve hospital and residential services by caring for people in their own homes. Department of Health and Social Service statistics had shown that this policy had brought about a drop in the length of time elderly people spent in hospital. The elderly spent an average of 105 days in hospital in 1972 this had fallen to 93.8 days in 1975 and 83.7 days in 1977. The pressure on domiciliary services due to this trend and the rise in the number of elderly persons was recognised and services to meet this situation were put forward as a priority and allowed to grow despite financial constraints.

The Government also attempted for the first time ever to set national levels for services. The standards were, Home Helps, 12 per 1,000 of the elderly population, 200 Meals on Wheels per 1,000 elderly, and 1 home nurse per 2,500 to 4,000 of the elderly population. These norms only served to highlight the very large differences in levels of services provided for the elderly by various Local Authorites.[10]

By 1976 the guidelines set by the Government had not been reached in all but one of the services. The home nursing service guideline of one nurse per 250,000 of the elderly had been reached. The home help service was 50 per cent short of the requirement. The meals on wheels service 54 per cent short. Day Centre places were 33-50 per cent short and geriatric hospital beds 14 per cent.

The special importance of the home help service in the support of the elderly was recognised and allowed to grow at the rate of 2 per cent per year, the chiropody service at 3 per cent per year and the meals on wheels service at 2 per cent per year. Assuming that the number of elderly persons would stay constant (instead of rising as at present) it was estimated that it would take many years to achieve these targets. The estimated time to reach the targets set in the Governments Consultative Document was estimated at 35 years for the home help service and 39 for the meals on wheels service.[11] Because of the variations in the level of services between the different Local Authorities and the low level of domiciliary services, provision for the elderly was given priority in any growth in services. The variations in expenditure by Local Authorities differed from £14,932 per 1,000 of the population to £8,586 on social services. The expenditure per 1,000 of the elderly population over 65 years of age varied from £28,809 to £14,006 to £2,323 to £ nill.[12]

Many Local Authorities cut back these services to the elderly despite being set as Central Government priorities. For example Somerset Social Services reduced the home help and meals on wheels service, Surrey County Council reduced day care for the elderly and increased meals on wheels charges and Dorset County Council reduced their home help service as did many other Social Service Departments.[13] This lack of control of Local Authority planning was an obvious flaw in the Government's ability to set and control the development of minimum national standards of service.

The doubts and criticisms of the time scales set in the first consultative document led to the publication of a further document in 1977 titled 'The Way Forward'. This paper also redefined the concept of community care. The concept was widened from care in the home to care of clients in community hospitals, hostels, day hospitals, residential homes and also covered the provision of domiciliary services in the clients own home, provided by the health services, local authorities and voluntary agencies. The new paper re-emphasised the urgent priority to be given to domiciliary services for the elderly. The document showed how far local authorities had to go to meet the minimum national standards. The short fall in residential places for the elderly was 6.9 places per 1,000 of the population and the shortfall in home helps was 5.5 whole time equivalents.[14]

The Labour Government in 1977 intended to publish a White Paper in 1979 on services for the elderly setting out a general strategy for service up to the end of the century. To help in the preparation of this plan the Ministry published a discussion document on services for the elderly in 1978 titled 'A Happier Old Age'.

This was an attempt to draw together the views of all interested parties as well as the views of elderly people themselves, which were contained in the research report 'The Elderly at Home' published that year.[15] The exercise brought to light some disturbing facts about the social work profession's attitude to the elderly. Most social work with the elderly was carried out by unqualified assistants without supervision by senior qualified staff. There was no condemnation of this situation or no statement by the social work profession about this terrible indictment of their attitude to provision of social work services for the elderly. The extension of the 'Good Neighbour Scheme' introduced in 1976 was called for. This scheme was introduced to help the two million elderly people who lived alone by encouraging their neighbours to interest themselves in their welfare and the development of practical help schemes.

The white paper on the elderly was published by the Conservative Government in 1981. This document 'Growing Older' had the same flaw as all its predecessors which was the implication that the services could only grow when economic resources would permit. This paper placed more emphasis on the provision of services by voluntary effort and the support of such effort by the statutory sector. The concept of community care was again changed from 'care in the community' to 'care by the community'.[16] What this meant was not spelt out and was typical of the use of the concept as a political expedient by governments to use the term to suit their own policies. No government has ever defined community care in concrete terms.

The white paper lacked a policy to cope with the increasing number of elderly and their changing needs. Services were listed and praised despite their inadequacy and shortfalls but no firm proposals were put forward. The paper was severely criticised by many agencies involved in working with and for the elderly. Apart from the idea to set up experimental nursing homes by Health Authorities the recommendations have had very little if any effect upon the development of services for the elderly since that date.

The reader, must not, because of my leaning towards domiciliary services for the elderly, believe that the period 1940 to 1980 was a continuum of growing appreciation of domiciliary services for the elderly. Much emphasis must be taken of the re-awakening of concern re demographic changes and growing restrictions on public expenditure. In the late 1960s, it was argued that the service should be generally available but by the middle of the 1970s, government documents, as we have seen were stressing the need for the setting of priorities, and value for money. Such general provision as luncheon clubs and visiting services lost popularity. Detailed investigation of every demand was the vogue of the day.

What effect did these attempts by various governments to develop services for the elderly in the 1970s have? The Black Report on 'Inequalities in Health'[17] published by the DHSS in 1980 and given very little publicity, pointed to a damning indictment of Government concern about health services, outlined many inadequacies in the various services for the elderly. Health service for the elderly was singled out as one service which had not been allowed to develop to its full potential. In particular dificiencies in Day Hospital Services and rehabilitation facilities for the elderly were noted. The report commented on the problem caused by the swing to treating the elderly at hone, rather than in hospitals, many people, because of this swing away from hospital care, felt the elderly were not getting access to the proper medical and nursing care. The report argued for more co-ordination and cooperation than existed. The report also advised a wider and more imaginative home care domiciliary service for the elderly. Has this happended? What is the state of domiciliary services for the elderly at the beginning of the 1980s?

Between 1951 and 1981 the overall elderly population increased by just under 50 per cent from 6,662,000 to 8,317,000 whereas the total number of elderly over 85 in this short period increased by nearly one hundred and fifty per cent from 217,000 to 568,000. Between 1951 and 2001 the elderly population over 85 will expand at over five and a half times the rate of the expansion of the general elderly population, and at over eight times that of the total population.

Moroney had pointed out in 1976 that by 2001 the total elderly population would rise by 27 per cent, the over 65's by 50 per cent, the over 75's by 82 per cent and the over 85's by a staggering 233 per cent.[18] The number of women surviving until the age of 75 is double the number of men. In 1981 the number of men between 65 and 74 years old was 2,220,000, and the number of women was 2,908,000, yet the number between 75 and 84 was 898,000 men compared with 1,728,000 women.

Women out number men 3 to 1 in the over 85 age range. Of all the women aged between 75 and 84, 53 per cent lived alone, and of those aged over 85, 49 per cent lived alone.

The elderly population in Great Britain as I

have pointed out has grown at a faster rate than the growth of the general population and the number of elderly people is expected to gradually increase to the year 2018.

The number of those aged over 75 is expected to decrease but it has been estimated that between 1901 and 2018 the number of elderly aged over 85 will have increased by 212 per cent.

Such a dramatic increase in life expectancy and reduction in mortality rates, would seem to reflect improved medical, social and environmental standards. Concomitant with these trends however, has been a growth in physical and mental illness of the elderly, particularly those in the older age groups, which in turn has, and will continue to place more pressure on the various medical and social services supporting the elderly in the Community.

Harris, in her study the 'Handicapped and Impaired in Great Britain', attempted to provide a set of figures which would give some indication of the problem. She defined the 'very severely handicapped' who totalled 116,000 elderly, as "those whose condition was such as to make them dependent on someone else for the performance of living activities which occur more than once a day". This group included those who were:-

(i) Mentally impaired or senile, unable to understand questions or give rational answers.
(ii) Permanently bed-fast.
(iii) Confined to a chair, unable to get in and out without the aid of another person.
(iv) Unable to feed themselves or need someone to assist them using the W.C.
(v) Doubly incontinent, or could not be left alone as they might harm themselves.

The severely handicapped elderly who numbered 215,000 were those who:-

(i) Experienced difficulty doing everything or found most things difficult, and some impossible.
(ii) Found most things difficult and three or four items difficult and some impossible.

The appreciably handicapped elderly number 380,000, and could do some things for themselves, but had difficulty with some items, and required assistance.

In terms of 1971 figures over half of all the elderly were found by Harris to be significantly impaired or handicapped, over 145,000 lived alone, approximately 215,000 lived with a spouse, approximately 265,000 lived with children and or spouse.

The living status of non-institutionalised elderly varied according to the severity of their handicap. Only 5.2 per cent of the very severely handicapped lived alone, yet over 23 per cent of the severe and appreciably handicapped did so. The number of severely handicapped is expected to rise over the next twenty years, particularly those over 75 years of age. Those over 75 will rise from 81 thousand to over one hundred thousand by the year 2001.

The number of very severely handicapped elderly is expected to grow by 26,500 in the forty years between 1971 and 2001. Assuming that a similar rate of growth of numbers of severely and appreciably handicapped can be expected (approximately 20 per cent), then by the year 2000 the number of elderly handicapped will have risen to approximately 143,900 people. It is also important to note that the number of very severely handicapped rises with age, and affects a greater percentage of the older age group. For a woman in the year 2001 the chance of being very severely handicapped will increase four-fold on her seventy-fifth birthday, whereas for men it will be a two-fold increase.

The average length of stay of elderly admissions to hospital declined. Between 1972 and 1977 an elderly person could expect his length of hospitalisation to be reduced by 20 per cent as shown earlier. These figures did not take into account whether the elderly patient left hospital dead or alive. However, total discharges and deaths amongst geriatric patients total 186,200 in 1972, and rose to 221,000 in 1976. This increase in the total number of patients took place at a time when the total number of geriatric beds available declined from 57,700 in 1972 to 55,700 in 1976.[19]

The implications of these trends are that, allowing for a proportionate increase in deaths amongth geriatric patients, elderly people are being admitted later into hospital than even six years ago, and being discharged earlier. Such a trend inevitably will place increasing pressure on the community based services supporting the elderly before and after discharge.

The number of visits to people over 65 by home nurses and health visitors increased significantly between 1971 and 1974, and since then has continued to rise more slowly each year.[20] The figures for both home nurses and health visitors only represent visits not numbers of clients, and as such may well be misleading. Such figures are open to two distinctly different interpretations. On the one hand the services may be supporting more clients, but less often or at about the same frequency as previously, or alternatively they could be supporting less clients, but visiting them more often. This latter interpretation further presumes that the clients they are visiting are the more severely handicapped, who require more attention. In terms of the proportion of each service allocated to the over 65's, it is possible to see that since 1974 about 15 per cent of health visiting capacity is regularly devoted to the elderly; similarly since 1975 the proportion of the Home Nursing Service attending elderly clients has remained more or less constant at about 40 per cent. The number of cases being attended by the Home Help Service has more than trebled between 1961 and 1980. In 1961 there were 249,000 elderly cases in England and Wales being attended; by 1972 this number had risen to 432,000, by 1978 had reached 652,000, and by 1980 this figure had risen to 704,000.[21]

However, such figures say nothing about the level of service provision. In fact, the rapid expansion of cases has been accompanied by a much slower increase in the number of Home Helps such that in 1958, one whole-time equavalent home help provided a service to an average of 4.1 cases whereas in 1972 one whole-time equivalent home help provided a service to 5.6 clients[22] and one home help to 12.6 cases by 1980 for Great Britain, but had fallen to one home help to 13.6 cases for England and Wales.

Both Health Visiting and Home Nursing Services have experienced similar trends in the ratio of manpower to elderly user ratio. In 1967 there was one full time home nurse for 55 elderly cases, whereas in 1971 that home nurse had to visit 64 cases. Moreover given that each full time home nurse in 1967 had 46 other cases under the age of 65, there was in fact, one full time home nurse for one hundred and one cases, 55 of which were elderly people. By 1971 each full time home nurse had a total of 116 cases, 64 of which were elderly people. Each health visitor in 1967 dealt with 63 elderly cases, in addition to her caseload under 65, and by 1971 the number of elderly clients rose to 72. Health Visitors spend most of their time with families and young children. The Home Nursing service however is primarily a service for the elderly. Over 80 per cent of their visits were to persons over 65 years in 1979 which was an increase from 71.5 per cent in 1968.[23]

Since 1971 and the implementation of the Local Authority Social Services Act which removed domiciliary services from the Health Department and the reorganisation of the Health Services in 1974 which brought the domiciliary nursing and chiropody services under the Health Authority there has been a very big drop in the percentage of time these services have spent supporting the elderly. In 1971 chiropodists spent 20 per cent of their time serving the elderly but in 1979 this had dropped to 10 per cent. District nurses spent 5 per cent of their time with the elderly in 1979 compared with 31 per cent in 1971. There was a similar drop in the support given by Health Visitors, 10 per cent in 1971 to 1.4 per cent in 1979. This large swing in domiciliary social health services has not been taken up to any great extent by domiciliary social services. The average number of visits by home helps to the elderly has stayed remarkably static since 1976 an increase of about 5 visits per elderly person on home help caseloads.

The extent of the community based social domiciliary services that I have described, has not meant that all handicapped elderly people automatically receive some form of assistance. In fact, 37 per cent of very severely handicapped elderly receive no welfare service at all. Harris estimated that in 1968 there were 2,000 very severely handicapped people, the vast proportion of whom are elderly, and 90,000 handicapped people (again the majority of whom are elderly), who lived alone, and received no welfare services. She further noted that there were 15,000 very severely handicapped elderly people, relying on equally elderly spouses, who received no welfare services.[24]

Home helps only visited 13.6 per cent of the very severely handicapped elderly, compared to 17.0 per cent of the severely handicapped elderly. This can possibly be explained by the much lower numbers of very severely handicapped elderly who live alone, 5.2 per cent compared with 23.7 per cent of the severely handicapped elderly. In absolute terms these percentages mean that only 94,126 handicapped elderly, out of a total of 711,000 received Home Help Service. This use of services by the elderly imply that families, relatives and neighbours are providing many of the basic services required by the handicapped elderly in particular.

Why is the emphasis now on care of the elderly in the community by family, friends or volunteers? How does this reliance on care by family and volunteers relate to the present reduction in services. There is now a return to the policies of the 1950s. It is as if we have not learned any lessons from the past thirty years. Townsend and Wedderburn in the fifties showed only too clearly the pressures placed upon families by elderly relatives. For many families this pressure was enormous and caused great strain upon the elderly person and the carer. It was clear from the research at that time that the family could not care for its most handicapped elderly. Slack at the end of the 1950s also showed that voluntary organisations were unable to provide adequate domiciliary services. This inability of voluntary organisations and family to support many of the elderly led Local Authorities to push for powers to provide the services themselves. The 1962 National Assistant Act and the 1968 Health Services and Public Health Acts were the result of this pressure.[25]

Summary

It can be deduced from the facts that I have put forward in this chapter that services for the elderly are still unco-ordinated, unplanned and vary in quality from Health and Local Authority Area. The split in the provision of domiciliary services for the elderly between health and social services in 1972 has meant that there has been uneven and unco-ordinated development of services with little or no evaluation of the effects upon each departments or agencies services. The majority of elderly persons in the community are still supported by the family or relatives. The rhetoric of various governments about services for the elderly has not been translated into concrete services. This rhetoric has meant nothing to those elderly who receive no/or an insufficient service. The 1970s have seen the Social Services cut, not expanded to meet increasing needs. The decade has seen services provided by insufficient and unqualified staff, assistant or junior staff. Cuts or standstills in services have possibly led to the early death of some old people. Eighty per cent of Local Authorities in England and Wales have cut their services or increased their charges for domiciliary services. These cuts must be seen in relation to the minimum standards set by the Government in the early 1970s which have not been met. The average recommended level of home helps per thousand of the elderly population was 12 but this figure in 1979 was only 7. The meals on wheels target had only been half met. The scene for the elderly in the community in the 1980s is very bleak indeed. No political party seems able or willing to put into practice a comprehensive policy for the elderly. Because of the importance of central government and the insensitivity of many Local Authorities this lack of community support to the elderly will be costly in terms of health and lives and will be terrible to behold. Despite these cuts many Local Authorities, as can be seen in chapters 4 and 5, are making attempts to provide an effective and efficient domiciliary service for the elderly.

Notes

1. DHSS, Priorities for Health and Personal Social Services in England (HMSO, London, 1976). DHSS, The Way Forward (HMSO, London, 1977). DHSS, Care in Action (HMSO, London, 1981). DHSS, Growing Older (Cd. 8137, HMSO, London, 1981).

2. DHSS, Care in Action, 1981.

3. DHSS, The Way Forward, 1977.

4. DHSS, Growing Older, 1981.

5. Numbers of home helps for the London Boroughs of Lambert and Hackney were not available. I have used 1974 staff figures for these boroughs in the 1979 figures.

6. Central Statistical Office, Social Trends 1972-1982 (HMSO, London, 1983).

7. DHSS, Review of the Home Help Service (HMSO, London, 1972).

8. DHSS Circular HC (77) 17, Joint Care Planning: Health and Local Authorities, 1977.

9. Ibid.

10. DHSS, Priorities for the Health and Personal Social Services (DHSS, 1976).

11. Whose Priorities? (Radical Statistics Health Group, Winchester, 1976).

12. Social Service Statistics, 1975/76. County Councils Gazette, Sept. 1975.

13. British Association of Social Workers. Press Releases, BASW 17 Dec. 1975 and 10 Oct. 1976.

14. DHSS, The Way Forward (HMSO, 1977).

15. DHSS, A Happier Old Age (HMSO, 1978).

16. DHSS, Growing Older (HMSO, 1981).

17. DHSS, Inequalities in Health (HMSO, 1980).

18. R.M. Moroney, The Family and the State (Longman, London, 1976), p.35.

19. DHSS, *Health and Personal Social Services Statistics* (HMSO, London, 1972-1977).
20. G.S.S., C.S.O. *Social Trends* (HMSO, London, 1979).
21. G.S.S., C.S.O. *Social Trends* (HMSO, London, 1977).
22. R.M. Moroney, *The Family and the State*, 1976.
23. Research Highlights, No. 3 (Aberdeen University, 1982).
24. A. Harris, *The Handicapped and Impaired in Great Britain* (O.P.C.S. Social Survey Division, HMSO, London, 1971) p.51.
25. K.M. Slack, *Councils Committees and Concern for the Old* (The Coldicote Press, London, 1960).

Chapter Four

SERVICES IN THE 1980s

In this chapter I will examine the work load of the Domiciliary Nursing and Social Services today. I will also discuss some of the most pertinent and urgent questions arising from that analysis, such as the role of the Nursing Auxiliary and the overlap with the work of the Home Help, the effect of charging for services and the problems caused by the lack of clear objectives for the various services. The developing role of the Domiciliary Care Organiser and the effect of this upon other personnel in the Social Services Department will also be examined.

In the last chapter it was shown how the Domiciliary Services have grown slowly to meet new and ever increasing demands. However this development has now slowed down because of Government policy as a reaction to the economic climate today. How has this worsening economic climate affected the development of Domiciliary Services for the elderly? A preliminary survey of Social Service Departments carried out by the Association of Directors of Social Services in 1979 showed that for 1979/80 savings envisaged were in the region of 30 per cent which was some £36 million. In many Local Authorities the cuts or savings were evenly spread across all services but three services suffered most, residential care, Home Help and Meals on Wheels. Many Authorities also introduced charges for the first time.

The past 15 years has seen a growth in community care facilities for the elderly in their own homes. Demand for such services continue to grow as other complementary services such as hospital care decreases. The policies of the present Conservative Government reinforces the demand for community care but economic policies are presenting difficulties, which are intensifying the suffering and distress of the elderly, who are the weakest and most vulnerable members of society. The report of the Association of Directors of Social Services for 1981 and 1982 only confirms this tragic trend. In 1981 they report almost half of one per cent cut in expenditure in real terms.

Despite these restrictions there are today more Home Helps and Meals on Wheels provided than ever before. The number of Community Nurses serving the elderly has also risen but has there been an increase in real terms or has the increase just kept pace with demands? The only reliable set of figures which tells the total number of staff employed in the Domiciliary Services in England and Wales was published in 1979 by the National Council of Home Help Services. The number of Domiciliary Organisers was 1,441 and home helps numbered 61,984. Each Organiser was responsible for approximately 47 home helps and 362 clients. Each home help supported about 7 clients. Most of the Organisers worked full time, 87 per cent, compared to only about 4 per cent of home helps.

The staffing ratios differ from region to region and Authority. The number of clients per Organiser varies from 304 in the English Counties to 485 in Wales and the number of staff that each Organiser has to manage differs from 38 in London to 77 in Wales. The turn-over of manual staff was much slower in the Welsh Counties at 11.5 per cent compared with 17.7 per cent per annum in the English Counties. Although there had been an increase in the total numbers of hours provided by the home helps, the number of hours per client has fallen from 132 per year in 1874/75 to 116.7 per year in 1980/81. The number of home help hours per person over 65 rose from 24 in 1974/75 to 27.4 in 1982/83.

What do 53,000 home helps do for their 718,000 clients? The tasks they carry out cover a very wide spectrum from domestic tasks like cleaning to basic nursing tasks such as washing and bathing. The trend in the past few years has been to develop a service which delivers a personal caring service with less and less emphasis on domestic tasks. However, the largest part of the job is still in the field of domestic tasks. This move to a total home care and personal care service but also with emphasis on the domestic role is to be welcomed. Home Helps in many instances are the only contact from the Social Services Department to work with the elderly and to limit their role to domestic tasks would deprive the elderly of a vital caring service that no other agency is prepared to offer. The role of the Domiciliary Services is today, more than ever, vitally important in the spectrum of care offered to the elderly. Some researchers and writers have expressed anxiety at this move to a more personal caring service but this is, in my view, not justified.[1] There is no evidence that this swing is unhelpful to the elderly. Not to use the interpersonal skills of the Domiciliary Worker would be an irresponsible act. The elderly need a service which encompasses many of their needs other than domestic tasks such as help with dressing, bathing, getting in and out of bed, dressing of minor wounds, shopping, representation at tribunals and service agencies, all tasks that trained Home Helps have carried out adequately.

The Coventry Project (see Chapter 5) is a very good example of the most adequate use of the domiciliary worker with the elderly. The workers were selected for their ability to undertake a wide variety of jobs such as assisting in the rehabilitation of physically handicapped clients, negotiating with other agencies on behalf of clients, and their ability to deal with problems on their own initiative and in emergencies. Other Local Authorities have realised the valuable contribution the domiciliary worker can make to the care of the elderly.

Cambridgeshire County Council in the late 1970s experimented with widening the role of the home help and calling them Domiciliary Care Assistants. Their role was not only to provide domestic support but also personal care and basic nursing for elderly clients who fell into that gray overlap area between Health and Social Service provision.[2] The Domiciliary Care Assistants were also expected to spend more time with clients than conventional Home Helps and to be available at critical times during the day and at weekends. Most of the clients they served were over 85 years of age and many over 90. This worker performed many tasks for the elderly person such as cooking, washing laundry, bathing clients, getting them in and out of bed, taking them for walks in the park and shopping. They also provided an important liaison link on behalf of the client and Department to mobilise services for their clients. The report of the project does point out that the amount of personal care and domestic tasks carried out by the staff should not obscure the tremendous amount of social and emotional support given also. As a result of their experience, Cambridgeshire Social Service Department are expanding this scheme and the role of the Home Help.

The assessment of the clients need for Domiciliary and review of those needs is vitally important as is the supervision of the staff providing the services. This aspect of the role of the Domiciliary Care Organisers has been widely discussed. Many Departments have not an adequate ratio of Organisers to Domiciliary Staff to supervise them adequately or assess or review clients needs. The number of home helps which an organiser can be responsible for supervising may vary from 109 in Gwynedd to only 7 in West Sussex. The average number for which an organiser is responsible is 48 home helps.[3] One result of this situation is a lack of supervision of the work of the home help so that quality or quantity of work cannot be observed or guaranteed to clients. Only one Local Authority has looked at the problem caused by this lack of quality control. This study examined the actual work allocated to the home help per client and the actual work carried out for the client.[4] Discrepancies between what Organisers asked to be done and what was carried out were discovered. What the authors were unprepared for was the scale of the differences. In one geographical area studies a difference in what was requested by the organiser and carried out by the home help was discovered in 70 per cent of cases. The reasons for this was placed at the Organiser's inability to supervise and to communicate to home helps their clients' needs clearly enough. The report also questioned the organiser's ability to assess the client's needs but it put forward that if need is to be properly assessed then adequate follow-up is also necessary.

This report highlights the difficulty of trying to find out on what criteria Organisers assess client need. "Home Help Organisers often argue that no systematic assessment review schedule can be as sensitive or accurate as the exercise of their 'intuition'".[5] This statement of Goldberg and Connely's is all too true. The author as both a manager of a Domiciliary Service for some years and now a teacher of Domiciliary Organisers and Social Services has experienced this attitude every time organisers are asked to examine their assessment techniques. Domiciliary organisers seem unable for some reason, perhaps because of their domination in the past by other prefessions, or lack of confidence or training, to discuss rationally this important aspect of their job. They are not helped in their tasks by the fact that very few Social Service Departments have a philosophy or written statement of objectives for their Domiciliary Services. Because of this lack of clear objectives or assessment criteria by either officers or councils, many Home Help Organisers continuously find themselves having to justify to councillors and others their reasons for the allocation or lack of support to certain clients. One way to counter this criticism of their work is to hide their reasons behind the 'magic' of intuition. Headly[5] in his review of the Home Help Service found that Home help Organisers were left complete discretion in their assessment and allocation of resources. Many of the studies however show that despite this lack of guidance there is a consistent approach to assessment of client's needs by organisers.[7] Two reports have however questioned this statement.

One of the reports, in 1970, came to the following conclusion:-

"Once the decision to allocate home help has been taken, the amount of help given is decided by the organiser by taking into account the physical needs of the patient, the type and condition of the dwelling and the possibility of other help being available. Practically all the assessments appear to be subjective: only two organisers (out of 54 interviews) worked to a scale and very few attempted a definition of 'needs'."[8]

The second report by Marks paid more attention to the question of allocation and appears to confirm a commonly held view about the service. "There is no obvious explanation for the variation in the service provided in differing areas of the same authority... As assessments made by organisers are not standardised and the time thought to be required is purely a matter of each organiser's personal judgement, it is probable that variation between areas is caused by differences in organisers' methods of allocation of time. Thus, the time allocated to each client must depend not only upon their 'needs' but also upon which organiser assesses them. This must raise serious doubts about the adequacy of the service being provided to individual clients. The results of the study also indicated that time allocated to recipients was not usually closely related to the circumstances (crudely measured) or characteristics of the clients."[9]

What do organisers assess their clients as needing? Table 4.1 shows that Home Helps spend a large proportion of their time cleaning and doing such tasks as shopping and other household chores. Despite the recent concern that the role of the home help might be changing to that of more personal care such as bathing, washing and feeding, this is not borne out by the evidence. From the limited data available on the tasks carried out by home helps it can still be argued that the service is one concerned with offering a practical service to elderly clients.

Table 4.1 Percentage of time Home Helps spend on tasks

Tasks	Hammer-smith 1974	Cumbria 1978	Avon 1976	Hilling-don 1977	Gwynedd 1977	Cheshire 1980	Devon 1979
Make tea, chat,etc.	4	15.2	2.8	-	-	-	-
Light Fire	4	14.7	2.7	0.5	6.7	3.2	-
Personal Tasks	6	6.8	8.0	-	1.7	1.2	2
Prepare/ cook meal	6	9.3	11.5	1.5	4.6	4.9	7
Change clients clothes	8	-	-	-	1.6	0.8	-
Laundry etc	12	28.0	15.3	9.4	15.9	18.9	12
Shopping/ Errands	19	26	13.9	14.7	10.8	24.2	22
Cleaning etc	41	-	45	72	45	39.9	59
Other	-	-	-	1.9	2.2	5.7	10

Source: Monitoring Home Help Assessments and Allocation L. B. Hammersmith 1974. Home Help Service in Cumbria, Cumbria C.C. 1978. Home Help Assessments, Avon S.S.D. 1976. Domiciliary Service Evaluation L. B. Hillingdon 1977. A Research Review of the operation of the Home Help Service in Gwynedd, Gwynedd C.C. 1977. Home Help Service in Cheshire, Cheshire C.C. 1980. Allocating the Home Help Service, Bedford Sq. Press, 1979.

It is clear from the limited research results to date that a high proportion of the work of the Domiciliary Home Help Service is oriented towards providing a domestic service.

What is the role of the managers of the service,

the Domiciliary Organiser? How is their time allocated amongst the different aspects of their job? The most important task of the Organiser is the assessment and review of client needs and the appropriate allocation of services to meet that need. Other important tasks are the recruitment and training of staff, allocation and supervision of work allocated to home helps and also the routine clerical and administrative tasks associated with the management of the service. The amount of time spent by organisers on these routine clerical tasks have been the subject of a number of studies. Many authorities have come to realise that the role of the organiser covers a wide variety of tasks. They have come to the conclusion that the responsibilities are too wide. One authority in particular[10] has examined this problem and tried to separate the professional responsibilities of the organiser from the routine clerical tasks that could be allocated to a more appropriate person, in order to release the organiser for her more important tasks. The survey 'Home Help Services in Great Britain' carried out in 1979 showed the wide spectrum of responsibities carried by organisers, such as, responsibility for Meals on Wheels Services, Meals on Wheels Kitchens, supervision of volunteers and supervision of Home Wardens. Also the number of staff an organiser may be responsible for can vary. Despite the responsibility for personnel and allocation of resources, many authorities have now realised that organisers are subject to very little control or supervision by senior staff or very little scrutiny of how they make assessments or allocate services.

In the County of Lothian 43 per cent of the organisers' time was spent on client and home help visiting and support, ie visiting clients 20 per cent, writing reports 57 per cent, liaison 8 per cent, recruitment 3 per cent, home help support only 5 per cent, and 15 per cent with administrative tasks in the office, but in the London Borough of Hillingdon in 1977 visiting clients took up only 18 per cent of the organisers' time and 25 per cent of the assistant organisers' time. The majority of the duties in Hillingdon were in the administrative area. One particular authority, prompted by the unequal distribution of resources in the County, the high referral rates, the amount of clerical work being carried out by organisers and the lack of reviews of client need, analysed what the organisers did and how they carried out their tasks. The Authority were also concerned that staff should control over 15 per cent of the department budget (over one million pounds) and were subjected to little supervision or control by senior staff.[11]

The investigation of the organisers role led to the conclusion that the responsibilities of the organisers were too heavy and recommends that the clerical and administrative tasks should be separated from the professional tasks. Even in this one Authority the responsibilities of the organisers varied. Some had responsibility for the management of 50 home helps, others 100. The number of clients served by organisers varied also from 275 to 530 per organiser. The review only highlighted the complexity of the role of the organiser. Because of the burden of office work the organiser was unable to review the needs of clients or supervise the work of the home helps. Communication with home helps as to their work load was inadequate as was the initial assessment of clients needs. Many organisers are reluctant to split off the administrative task and concentrate on their professional role of assessment, review and supervision of staff. Why this should be so is not clear from the research so far. The author, in many interviews with organisers, can only offer a subjective opinion. Many organisers are untrained and feel very insecure when questioned about how they carry out assessments and reviews of clients and also how and upon what grounds they allocate resources to particular clients. This inferiority complex will only disappear when there is a proper training programme for staff and a fully trained service is attained.

The relationship between organisers and other colleagues in the Social Service Departments differs from area to area. In the City of Coventry the organiser is seen as a valuable member of the Social Services team. However, organisers are becoming more and more isolated as social workers delegate the responsibility for the elderly to untrained staff and social work assistants. The low priority given to the elderly by social workers may contribute to the friction between the two groups of staff and the lack of communication between them. Only 3 per cent of home help staff would consult a social worker if they needed advice about a client.[12] Home Help Organisers are concerned by "the increasingly accepted view by social workers that the elderly never need 'casework'. That their situation must always be eased by the intention of practical assistance (vis-a-vis home help etc) or by clients removal to part III accommodation."[13] This antagonism towards social workers which is so obvious from the Institute of Home Help Organisers' evidence to the Enquiry into the roles and tasks of the Social Worker (Barclay Report) in 1982 that the relations between Domiciliary Services and social workers leaves a lot to be desired. Many other workers have also pointed out this deplorable state of affairs in the past few years.[14]

Goldberg and Connelly have put forward views as to the most appropriate person in the Social Service Departments to be responsible for the assessment of clients' needs and allocation of resources.[15] They argue that social workers have a central and vital contribution to play in performing this role because of their diagnostic skills. All the evidence points to the fact that in the area of working with the elderly the only group of workers with the experience, knowledge and skills to carry out this task are the Domiciliary Care Organisers. As far as the care of the elderly is concerned the lack of concern by social work staff for their wellbeing, the lack of knowledge and experience of working with the elderly, all point to the Domiciliary Care Organiser being the most appropriate member of the Social Service Department to carry total responsibility for the care of the elderly in the Community.

Community Domiciliary Nursing

The type, number and work of the Community Nurse has changed over the past twenty to thirty years. The organisation and provision of service has also changed. There is now increased emphasis on nursing care in the community and the corresponding concern re the best possible use of appropriate skills of qualified nursing staff. Since 1962 concern has been expressed about the amount of time spent by qualified nursing staff on non or routine nursing tasks.[16] The need to review the organisation of Local Authority Nursing Services so that qualified staff were deployed to make the best possible use of their expertise was emphasised by the Ministry of Health in 1968 and 1972.[17] The Home Nursing Service today is made up of different grades of staff each having a distinct role in the care of the patient. The service comprises State Registered Nurses who have completed a special course (District Nursing), State Enrolled Nurses, Nursing Assistants and Nursing Auxiliaries. The District Nurses as distinct from the Health Visitors spend most of their time caring for elderly patients. Health Visitors in 1971 visited five and a half million cases of whom 10 per cent were elderly, this had risen to 15 per cent by 1978, but in 1980 this percentage fell to 13 per cent. Home Nurses on the other hand visited 1,265 million cases in 1971, 54 per cent were elderly but this percentage had droped to 43 in 1980 although the total number of cases visited had risen to 3,765 million.

The first major attempt to study the work of the District Nursing Service was by Hockey in 1965.[18] She surveyed the work of the nurses in six selected districts. She was amongst the first to point out that nurses spent comparatively little time in direct contact with patients. She found that in 1965 District Nurses spent only 60 per cent of their time with patients, this had actually dropped to below 50 per cent in 1982.[19] One of the most disturbing findings was the appalling lack of knowledge by Doctors of the work, training or qualifications of their nursing colleagues. Hockey carried out a second study of Community Nursing Services in 1972.[20] By 1972 the average Local Authority Nurse was on the whole married, 40-49 years of age and many had been in the Service for over ten years. They spent much of their eight hour working day on travelling and only 40 per cent of their time on direct patient care, a drop of 20 per cent since 1965. The Service supported many more women than men. This figure in 1982 was 47 per cent of direct patient care time with women compared to 2.7 per cent with men for District Nurses. Nursing Auxiliaries on the other hand spent far more time with women as much as 64 per cent of their time and 3.5 per cent with men.

Many of the elderly women attended were on the whole in the older age bracket than men. Over 15 per cent of patients were bedfast and required almost complete attention to their physical needs. The frequency that basic nursing care tasks were carried out in one week, out of a total of 8,502 basic activities carried out by qualified nurses was routine care or bed bath 3,673 (43.2 per cent), bathing in a big bath 394 (4.6 per cent), care of the hair, nails, feet 1,613 (18.9 per cent), assisting with bed pan, commode etc. 1.243 (14.6 per cent), taking TPR 718 (8.4 per cent and rehabilitative exercises 816 (9.5 per cent).

The survey did point out the confusion and anomalies surrounding the employment of State Enrolled Nurses. Guidance as to their work and responsibilities was either outdated or non existant. None of Hockey's work, however, examined the important aspect of quality and standard of care given by either the qualified Nurses or Assistants or Auxiliaries.

As early as 1965 it had been recognised that a rigid allocation of duties according to qualification or grade was not possible.[21] The Standing Nursing Advisory Committee of the Central Health Services Council in 1965 put forward the necessity to form a new grade of Nurse to relieve the qualified Nurse of routine duties. This new grade of "Nursing Auxiliary" could do the basic nursing such as bathing, washing, foot hygiene, dressing, undressing of patients under the supervision of the qualified Nurse. Local Authorities were advised to undertake studies of their methods of working with a view to employing Auxiliary Nurses.[22] The use of this unqualified Nurse it was thought would not lead to any deterioration of patient care as they would be under the constant supervision of a qualified Nurse. The duties and training of Auxiliary Nurses was the topic of a second advisory circular in 1970 and again in 1971.[23] Nursing Auxiliaries were, by 1977, valued members of the Nursing team.[24] The Auxiliary was felt to be able to carry out the following duties for patients in the Community:-

Assisting in the preparation of the patient's home on discharge from hospital.

Weighing patients, assisting with making beds, help patients to make and prepare meals and to assist in the service of those meals.

Help with feeding patients.

Assist with bathing in bed and in the bathroom, with the lifting, turning and moving of patients.

Help patients with personal hygiene, including care of the hair, teeth and nails.

Participate in the rehabilitation of patients in the home.

Dressing, undressing, taking to the toilet and using sani-chairs and commodes.[25]

Many Health Districts today have their own view of the role and appropriate tasks which can be undertaken by Auxiliaries. Most of them include the basic nursing care tasks and supervision by qualified staff. To advise nursing managers and to provide guidelines the Maplin Committee Nursing Sub-Group in 1982 issued a definition of the nursing auxiliary and a description of the tasks she could be expected to carry out. The committee did, however, recognise that due to local circumstances their responsibilities would differ from Authority to Authority. A working group of the United Kingdom

Central Council for Nursing, Midwifery and Health Visiting on education and training in 1982 deplored the confusion and exploitation of Assistant and Auxiliary Nurses and recommended that the titles should be abolished and the term 'Care Assistant' substituted. In 1982 over 11 per cent of Community Nursing Staff were of this grade and 99 per cent were female.[26]

The latest survey to examine the role of Community Nurses was carried out by the Office of Population Censuses and Surveys for the Department of Health and Social Security in 1980 and published in 1982.[27] This study was of a random sample of 24 Health Districts Community Nursing Staff. Over one third of Community Nurses employed are Health Visitors and one fifth are Midwives and District Nurses. Nursing Auxiliaries and the School Nursing Service formed another 10 per cent. Many of the Nurses spent a large proportion of their time travelling and on non nursing duties. Nursing Auxiliaries spent the highest proportion of their time in direct contact with patients. Most of these patients were elderly.

Table 4.2 shows that two thirds of the nurses fell into the 30-50 age group and are predominantly female with more men in the District Nursing category than any other. Nursing Auxiliaries and Geriatric Nurses had a large percentage of their numbers who had been in the job between one to ten years. District Nurses and Health Visitors had one fifth of their number in the job for over fifteen years.

Health Visitors spend 62 per cent of their time with children and only 9 per cent with the elderly. The District Nurse on the other hand spends most of her time with the female patients who are over sixty-five years of age. Nursing Auxiliary staff spend 64 per cent of their time with female patients over sixty-five and 88 per cent of their direct contact time in supporting the elderly. This can be further broken up in to the amount of time spent with male and female patients. District Nurses spend 47 per cent of their time with females over 65 compared with Auxiliary Nurses who spend 64 per cent and Health Visitors 8 per cent. Only 2.7 per cent of District Nurses spent any time with men who were over 65 compared with 24 per cent by Auxiliary Nurses and 3.5 per cent by Health Visitors.

What do Nurses do when they are with patients? District Nurses spend 40 per cent of their time carrying out technical procedures such as giving injections, changing dressings and inserting and removing stitches. Nursing Auxiliaries spend a large proportion of their time on the personal care of the patient. The District Nurse spends 40 per cent of her time on basic nursing care and the Nursing Auxiliary 85 per cent of her time. The Health Visitor on the other hand spends 73 per cent of her time offering advice and counselling and only 4 per cent of her time on basic nursing care.

Table 4.2 Type of Nurse by Age, Sex, Marital Status and length of time in Job.

	Nursing Auxiliary	District Nurse	Health Visitor	Geriatric Nurse
Age				
20 - 29	4%	15%	12%	2%
30 - 39	35%	33%	26%	31%
40 - 49	37%	34%	36%	37%
50 - 59	21%	17%	24%	28%
60+	3%	1%	1%	2%
Sex				
Female	99%	96%	99%	98%
Male	1%	4%	1%	2%
Marital Status				
Married	85%	76%	66%	80%
Single	3%	13%	24%	14%
Widowed	6%	3%	3%	2%
Divorced	6%	6%	5%	4%
Separated	-	2%	2%	-
Time in Job				
Less 1 year	16%	12%	10%	23%
1 - 9 years+	74%	65%	57%	64%
10 - 14 years+	8%	12%	13%	7%
15 years+	2%	11%	20%	6%
Number of Nurses (=100%)	609	824	1057	44

Source: Nurses Working in The Community, 1980, (HMSO 1982).

Many of the studies of the Community Nursing Services highlight the problem of confusion about the role of the Nursing Auxiliary, the volume of work and the amount of non nursing duties carried out by qualified staff. New demands are being made of staff but it is not clear if these demands are coming from patients or because of the organisation of the services such as the introduction of Nursing Auxiliaries and the changing pattern of attachment of nurses to General Practitioners. The role of the Nursing Assistant or Auxiliary can only be justified if their work is allocated and supervised by qualified staff.

One study and the only one to examine this problem, found that despite Ministry advice there was no evidence to support the claim that Nursing Auxiliaries were supervised.[28] This raises questions of the accountability of these staff and the quality of their work.

Meals on Wheels

Meals on Wheels constitute one of the most important and major forms of Community Support to the elderly wishing to stay in their own homes. In line with other support systems they have been extended in recent years to help maintain the elderly in their own homes or to delay admission to hospital or residential care. Despite the importance of this service very little research into the effectiveness or efficiency of the service have been carried out. A recent study has, however, examined the organisation of a Meals on Wheels system, the cost and the relationships between need and provision, and the consumer reaction to the service.[29]

Providing food for the sick and elderly has a long history. In the beginning of the 20th century food and its nutritional value caused concern. The food given to the Army during the First World War was considered a much higher standard of feeding than ever before even when rationed.[30] One of the first Meals on Wheels service was organised and managed by the W.V.S. towards the end of the Second World War. Many believed that the dietary benefits received from the Civic Restaurants set up during the War could be continued by providing the meals to the housebound elderly at home. The service set up then, is much the same today except that there is a bigger proportion of statutory provision. The 1948 National Assistance Act allowed Local Authorities to subsidise the cost of providing the service to Voluntary Agencies. This Act was amended in 1962 to allow Local Authorities either to provide the service themselves or subsidise Voluntary Agencies to do so. Since 1962 when Local Authorities were allowed to provide the service themselves there has been an increase in choice and types of meals available to clients on a small scale.

The service has grown at a fast rate since 1962. In 1960 only 20,595 persons received meals. The W.V.S. was responsible for the provision of the majority of meals with the Local Authority providing a service to 537 people. The service did not operate on seven days nor was there a standard number of meals served. Many of the schemes closed for the Summer Holidays. One in five schemes operated on one day a week only and only one in four provided meals on four days or more a week.[31]

In 1960 the average number of meals per thousand of the population over sixty-five was 1.93 per week. By 1978 this had risen to 26.6 meals per thousand of the elderly population and to an average of 3.1 meals per week. The service has grown considerably. A total of over eleven million meals were served to clients in their own homes in 1967. This had risen to over sixteen million in 1972, twenty-six million in 1976 and over twenty-nine million in 1980. The number of meals served in day centres etc. rose from fifteen million to forty-four million in 1980. However "to talk of a policy for Meals on Wheels would be to stretch the meaning of that word to the limits. For whilst it is true to say Meals on Wheels have become, with Home Helps, the best known and most extensive Domiciliary Social Service to older people and have figured for some years in Government guidelines, they have never been the subject of serious political debate of National or Local Government."[32] Because of this fact the diversity of policies and practices vary widely and tend to be a combination of local provision and different relationships between Local Authorities and voluntary bodies. The variation in provision can differ from 1,000 meals per 10,000 of the population in Sheffield in 1978/79 to well over 14,000 per 10,000 of the population in the London Borough of Tower Hamlets.[33] The amount spent per meal can vary from 4.2p in the County of Essex to 25.4p in the London Borough of Lewisham.[34]

Like both the Home Help and Domiciliary Nursing Services the extent, quality and quantity varies enormously from Authority to Authority. The need for meals is, however, related to the number of aged and disabled living on their own. The prosperous elderly are just as likely to need the service as those on Supplementary Benefit. Unlike the Home Help or Nursing Service there is no private sector providing a service to those who need the service and can pay for it.

The Meals service is overwhelmingly a service to the elderly. Hunt in 1978 found that only 2.6 per cent of those over sixty-five received the service but this proportion increased with age so that 11 per cent of those over 85 years received the service. A recent survey in the City of Leeds shows that over 20 per cent of elderly people receive the service but the delivery of the service can still vary from region to region.[35]

As with other Domiciliary Services their effectiveness can only be judged if the services are directed to those persons in most need. In order to make sure that those in need are getting the service it is essential to identify the objectives of the service and the criteria for provision. The assessment of client need is at present carried out by many and varied grades of staff, most of them without any training in assessing client need. Many Home Help Organisers assess the need for the service in England and Wales and are also responsible for the management or co-ordination of the service.

The Leeds Study found that 33.7 per cent of recipients were assessed by social workers and 16.3 per cent by Welfare Officers. The 1979 National survey and the Leeds study indicate what Goldberg and Connelly call "a picture of a service where such detailed consideration of alternatives at the point of referral is rare, where systematic assessment and the balancing of one persons need against anothers is virtually absent and where re-assessment seldom occurs".[36] This chaotic situation has arisen despite advice from Ministry Officials in 1970[37] which offered clear and concise workable criteria re assessment of need. The Ministry circular suggested that persons living alone, the sick, mentally confused, physically handicapped and those with inadequate facilities would most need the service. The advice also stressed the need for regular reassessment. This advice has not been followed by staff, many are unaware of the existence of the circular. Many volunteers who provide the service feel that they cannot say no to clients.[38] In recognising this dilemma of volunteers circular 5/70 stresses that assessment and re-assessment should be carried out by Local Authority Staff.

Many needs of the elderly are met by the

service, but what is not clear from the studies is the importance of these needs and the effectiveness of current services to meet these needs. Circular 5/70 made clear that Meals on Wheels could only make a significant contribution to the nutritional needs of the elderly if provided on five days a week or more. Today few schemes provide this level of service. The evaluation of nutritional adequacy of meals is however problematical. "It is not surprising that there are regular reports of unbalanced or deficient nutrition in the Country, not that they should occur most often amongst the least financially or educationally privileged, that is to say, among the aged".[39] The study of the meals service in Scotland in 1976 pointed to the above fact. Studies have shown the lack of nutritional value of Meals on Wheels[40] and the latest study in Leeds supports this statement. This study was the first to assess the nutritional needs of a number of elderly people and found that many who received the service were not in need of nutritional supplement or at risk. Other studies have, however, showed that many old people suffer from anaemia.[41] Other indicators that old people were in need of some form of nutritional supplement is that in 1965 over 16 million prescriptions for vitamins and other nutritional items were prescribed by doctors.[42] These conflicting findings raise important questions about the identification and assessment of client need for meals. Are the appropriate clients receiving the service?

The Meals on Wheels service can be utilised as an opportunity for social contact to prevent isolation but studies show that the opportunities for this are minimal. Studies point out that if those who deliver the meals were allowed to spend even a few extra minutes with clients the time element would be prohibitive. The Leeds study agreed that "where social support is the object it is particularly important that assessment of the need for the aid is carried out and matched appropriately".[43] One study in Scotland showed that the average length of the time an organiser spent with recipient was 3-5 minutes.

The Meals on Wheels service provides a number of services, therefore, for the elderly, nutrition, social contact and surveillance. The service can also improve the morals of the elderly. Provision of a meal can help to sustain and encourage the elderly person to maintain other less demanding self-care activities.

The service today is therefore primarily a service to the elderly and the largest group of recipients are the over 75 year olds. In Harris' study in 1960 over 85 per cent of the recipients were over 75 and in a recent study in a London Borough the same percentage was found to be receiving the service.

In the Leeds study the majority of those receiving the service were over 80 years of age. Many of the recipients of the service live alone and are housebound. Many do also receive the support of other Domiciliary Services such as Domiciliary Nursing and Home Help.

The major areas of concern for the future of the service are in the field of assessment, nutritional value of the meals and frequency of provision. Research must be carried out on the development of adequate assessment criteria and the training of staff to assess client need. The objective of the service must be clarified for this to happen. Is the service one of providing a meal to those who need it, or a surveillance service or social contact service? Until it has been clarified which of these is the primary objective, there will continue to be an ineffective service.

Charging

I have included comment on charging policies because of their effect upon the development of the service. It is also necessary to look at charging to examine its effect upon the client and in many cases the client's family. The amount recovered by charging is small compared to the cost of collection. Charging must therefore be seen as a political tool and the result of Government and Local Policy rather than an economic method to reduce cost. Charging can also be seen as a method of introducing the privatisation of social services by rationing public services, thus forcing the elderly to turn to the private sector. This again is a return to the policies of the late 1940s. The concern then was to protect public funds rather than a desire to introduce privatisation of services, but the effect upon clients is much the same. They either do not get a service or they buy it from the private sector. This attempt to place the responsibility for the care of the elderly back upon the community is to be deplored. The Governments decision to stop supplementing the income of those elderly who have to pay for public sector services increases the pressure for the elderly to make use of the private sector as they would be allowed to claim a supplement for any payment to private domestic help approved by the Supplementary Benefit Commission. This decision has caused many hardships to clients.

Government advice to Local Authorities on charging for Domiciliary Services, in particular Meals on Wheels, is contained in circular 5/70 "The general practice is to make a fixed charge for meals well below cost. It is important that any charge should not be so high as to deter elderly people from accepting all the meals they need".[44] The Domiciliary Home Help Service has always been a service for which recipients could be made to contribute to the cost. The Nursing Services have never been subjected to such policies even when part of the Local Authority Health Service.

Section 29 of the National Health Service Act gives Local Authorities the power to charge for the service, having regard to the means of the persons being charged. The Minister advised in 1948 "that the standard charge per hour, or per day shall not exceed the actual cost - including wages, insurance, allowances for travelling time, retaining fees (if paid) and organisational and clerical expenses - to the authority".[45] Each Local Authority is allowed to determine its own charging policy within that broad criteria which allows for wide variations in policies between authorities. The 1974 Local Government Act allowed Local Authorities complete autonomy to introduce a charging system without Ministerial approval.

The variety of Local Authority policies relating to charging are numerous. Some Authorities offer a free service to every client, others only to supplementary benefit recipients, some have a flat rate charge for the service irrespective of level of service provided, some charge for each visit or operate a financial assessment scale for services. Most Authorities charge a flat rate per meal. Many Authorities offer a free service arguing that the collection of costs may exceed income. Hunt in 1970 found that only 9.5 per cent of the gross cost of the service was recovered. This had fallen to 4.3 per cent in the financial year 1975/76 and 4.4 per cent in 1979. Charges recovered in 1979 amounted to over 8 per cent in the English Non Metropolitan Counties, 1.9 per cent in Wales and 5.6 per cent in Scotland. The London Boroughs only received 1.4 per cent and the Metropolitan Districts 2.5 per cent. The average of all Authorities was 4.4 per cent.

The total budget for the Home Help Service for 1978/79 was £117.6 millions which was equivalent to about £2.92 per head of population. The recovery of charges was in the region of £5.2 million which was equivalent to about 13p. per head of the population. Most persons, in fact, receive the service free. Hunt in 1967 found that clients in receipt of supplementary benefit paid no charges in over 68 per cent of County Councils, nearly 78 per cent of County Boroughs and over 76 per cent of London Boroughs.

In 1967 recipients of the service in County Councils were more likely to have to pay for the service as compared with County Boroughs and London Boroughs. In general the more hours a client received the more they paid but very few elderly persons made a contribution even though they were receiving more support. 72.6 per cent of the elderly got the service free. By 1979 free services were provided by 88.8 per cent of Local Authorities to recipients of supplementary benefit.

Many of those Authorities providing a free service did not review either charges or client need. In Authorities not providing a free service client need and charges were reviewed annually but some authorities reviewed services every six months. In 1979, 25 English Counties reviewed their services annually, another 4 did so every six months. Only 5 of the London Boroughs looked at their charges annually but in 1979 only 7 out of the 32 London Boroughs charged for home help services. 19 Metropolitan Counties reviewed charges every year.

Many Authorities increase their charges annually for Domiciliary Services above the rate of inflation which in turn puts increasing pressure on the financial resources of the elderly. Because of the cuts in public expenditure and the need for Authorities to increase income many are for the first time introducing charges or putting costs up well above the level of inflation. (See Table 4.3). In 1981/82 over 42 Authorities put their charges up over 40 per cent and 3 introduced charges for the first time.

Table 4.3 shows that many of the changes in charging policies were in the home help services. The majority of Authorities who increased their charges increased them by well over the rate of inflation. Over 20 Authorities increased charges by over 60 per cent.

Although the cost of recovering Home Help charges has dropped from 12 per cent of the total cost to 4 per cent from 1960 the amount recovered from meals on wheels charges has grown. Table 4.3 shows that only 4 of the Authorities surveyed by the Association of Directors of Social Services in 1982 provide a free service.

Table 4.3 Percentage changes in charges made for Home Help and Meals on Wheels From pre-April 1980 - post-April 1981. England and Wales

L.A. Area	Service	Charge for 1st time	Free Service	No Charge	1-20%	20-40%	40-60%	60%+
London Borough	M.O.W.	0	0	0	1	4	9	8
Met Districts	M.O.W.	0	0	0	4	7	7	5
Non Met Counties	M.O.W.	0	0	0	7	6	9	7
London Boroughs	Home H.	0	8	2	0	5	7	1
Met Districts	Home H.	1	3	4	4	5	3	1
Non Met Counties	Home H.	2	1	3	6	10	7	3

Source: The effects of changes in personal social services expenditure for elderly people. ADSS 1982.

Judge and Matthews showed how the proporation of costs of meals on wheels fluctuated between 1972 and 1976. The amount recovered in 1972/73 was 19 per cent, 1973/74 17.6 per cent, 1974/75 15.8 per cent and 1975.76 this had risen to 18 per cent.[46]

A major area of concern over the increasing tendency of Authorities to recover the cost of providing services is the effect of this policy on elderly persons on low income or supplementary benefit. The Supplementary Benefit Authority now does not refund the amount a person on benefit may contribute to the Local Authority. The charge has now to be carried directly by the elderly person out of their income.

What effect has this increasing trend for Authorities to either introduce charges or increase them have upon the consumers? Judge and Matthews in 1977 looked at the effect of charges upon the elderly recipients of Domiciliary Services. As a result of the introduction of a flat rate charge

3-3.3 per cent of persons receiving the service cancelled as a result of the charge of 50p and in another Authority over 8 per cent terminated the service as a result of a flat rate charge of £1. Many of the clients who cancelled the service were felt by the organisers to be in essential need of the service and only 47 per cent of these clients could cope with the loss of the service although they would suffer considerable hardship. One or two Local Authorities themselves have examined the problems faced by clients who cancel the service as a result of the introduction of charges. Hunt in her survey of the Home Help Service in 1969 found that a small percentage of clients who have to pay for the service will restrict, themselves, the number of hours they receive from the Home Help Service. Over 7 per cent of the elderly agreed to pay full cost for the service rather than fill in a financial assessment form.[47] The assessment policies of the Authorities determine the amount, if any, of costs that elderly people have to contribute and the numbers and percentages who get a free service differs from Authority to Authority. (See Table 4.4)

Table 4.4 Percentage of Persons who pay for Domiciliary Service

Authority	Pay	Free
Cumbria C.C.(1978)	17.7%	82.3%
Cheshire C.C.(1980)	25%	75%
L.B. Redbridge (1980)	21.6%	78.4%
Derbyshire C.C. (1981)	100%	-
L.B. Ken. & Chelsea (1981)	31%	69%
Hunt (1969)	44.4%	55.6%
Gwynedd C.C. (1977)	10%	90%

Source: The Home Help Service in Cumbria 1978. Home Help Service in Cheshire 1980. The Home Help Service Redbridge 1980. Derbyshire and L. B. Kensington and Chelsea see Charging for the Home Help Service, 1982. Hunt 1970. A research review of the operation of the Home Help Service in Gwynedd 1977.

Before I discuss the effects of charging, it is necessary to understand that the majority of Domiciliary Services' clients are elderly and many of them are in receipt of supplementary benefit from the Department of Health and Social Security. This benefit is a supplementary benefit to bring the recipients income up to a level of just above the poverty line. Hunt found in 1969, which was before the DHSS decided to change their policy, that many elderly people had their costs refunded in part or full by the Supplementary Benefits Commission. A large percentage of the elderly receive either their old age pension and/or supplementary benefit.

Over 93 per cent of those who received home help were in receipt of old age pension, 65 per cent received Supplementary Benefit and 17 per cent had a private pension. Only 1.2 per cent were in receipt of a wage or salary.

It is clear that many elderly people are supported by Supplementary Benefit. These elderly people are the least able to pay for the services. Advice from the Minister of Health in 1968 to Local Authorities made the proviso re charges "the amount of any charges is not to be such that the recipient would need, because of it, to seek Supplementary Benefit".[48] The effect of this advice was reflected in the drop in the number of persons claiming Supplementary Benefit for assistance with home help charges, 20,000 in 1972 to 3,000 in 1975.[49] Since 1980 the Supplementary Benefit Regulations specifically preclude the payment of an additional payment for Local Authority Home Help. This rule does not apply to the payment for private home help. Local Authorities have been advised not to make charges to clients on Supplementary Benefit.[50] Many Authorities, as shown, have disregarded this advice and, indeed, many Authorities are introducing charges for the first time. The London Borough of Redbridge introduced a flat rate charge of £1.50p which affected 1,000 clients most of them elderly. Cheshire County Council also introduced a flat rate charge of £1.00 per week in an effort to reduce expenditure.[51]

At present there is also, in most Authorities, a flat rate charge per meal on wheel. There is relatively little evidence to show what effect these charges have upon clients and other services such as community nursing service. Costs have an effect upon the demand for services. Because of costs clients may not apply for services or stop or cut the services they receive. There is no evidence to show that it is the clients who do not need the service who withdraw. Hunt found that many staff felt that clients are debarred from applying for the services or gave them up because of the cost.[52]

A survey of consumer opinion by Cheshire Social Services Department in 1981 points out that 15 per cent of clients interviewed were not prepared to pay a recently introduced charge. 43 per cent of those clients who would refuse to pay said they could not manage without the service and had no idea what they were going to do or how they would get support for the cancelled service.[53] In the London Borough of Redbridge after the introduction of a flat rate charge for Domiciliary Services in 1980, about 10 per cent of clients cancelled the service. The report states that these 10 per cent tended to be the less 'needy' when looked at in terms of health and handicap, need for emotional support and social isolation. This type of effect was also found in the study by Judge and Matthews in Bradford. They also found that marginal need cases tended to give up the service when charges were introduced.

The Redbridge study does, however, point out that many of the clients receiving the service and who were on Supplementary Benefit were under severe financial strain and had to absorb the extra cost of the services by cutting down on such things as food and heating. A most dangerous thing for elderly people to do.[54]

Many of the studies show that those clients getting the service free tend to get more hours service than those who pay. In Cumbria paying clients received on average an hour less per week. The same phenomenon was found in a study of the service in Devon, and Cheshire.[55] Evidence from these studies point to charging being a break upon demand. Substitutes for the cancelled service were found to be not readily forthcoming. The Redbridge study found that neither family or volunteer support was available to those who cancelled. The difficulties of involving families and volunteers in supporting the elderly is well pointed out in a recent study of elderly support systems in Surrey.[56]

Charges raise more questions than they answer for Authorities. What type of client is deterred from receiving the service? What happens to those clients who cancel services because of cost? Should the elderly receive a free service? What is the knock-on effect of the elderly not being supported in the community, on nursing and medical services?

Summary

The 1980s have seen Local Authorities consolidate their existing domiciliary services but a few have, despite financial constraints, made attempts at innovation. Many of the problems experienced by Authorities in the 1970s have in the 1980s become more pressing. The changing role of the domiciliary service manager has only served to highlight many areas of concern. A number of research reports point to the trend for Home Help Organisers and District Nurses to spend more and more of their working day in carrying out routine clerical and administrative tasks and less and less time in direct contact with clients.

The differing levels of responsibility carried by organisers and the effect of this upon their work and the staff they supervise was discussed. The lack of supervision of the work of the home help and the community auxiliary nurse has been mentioned in a number of reports and given cause for concern to the managers of the services. No study to date has looked at the effects upon the client of this lack of supervision. This problem and the area of assessment of client need are two areas in which research is most needed. The tasks carried out by domiciliary care staff for clients varies from authority to authority but in general the role of these workers is widening to encompass a bigger range of personal caring tasks, many of which are not within their job descriptions. One home help, in a letter to the author, typified this attitude of home helps and their relationship with clients, "I would like to make a personal point as a home help. The clients I help can have many different needs. I am prepared to do almost any job, especially for the older person who finds things difficult".

The overlap in roles of the home help and community auxiliary nurse needs to be closely monitored if duplication of effort and waste of resources is to be avoided. The late 1970s and early 1980s have seen a disturbing trend for Local Authorities to either introduce for the first time charges or increase their existing charges for domiciliary services. Few studies have examined the effects of this policy upon clients or their families. It is all the more important that this area of concern should be analysed in view of the policy of the Supplementary Benefit Commission to stop supplementing the income of those clients who have to pay charges to Local Authorities. This policy does not however apply to those clients who pay private agencies for home help approved by officers from the Commission.

The late 1970s has seen a period of retrenchment by many Local Authorities, but a few have tried to introduce new methods of service delivery. Some of these innovations I discuss in Chapter Five.

Notes

1. E. Goldberg and N. Connelly, The Effectiveness of Social Care for the Elderly (Heinemann Educational Books, London, 1982).

2. K. Simons and R. Warburton, A Sensible Service (Cambridge County Council, Cambridge, 1980).

3. The Home Help Service in Great Britain (National Council of Home Help Services, Cambridge, 1979).

4. D. Gwynne and L. Fean, Home Help Service in Cumbria (Cumbria Social Service Department, Cumbria, 1978).

5. E. Goldberg and N. Connelly, The Effectiveness of Social Care for the Elderly, p.58.

6. R. Hedley and A. Norman, Home Helps: Key Issues in Service Provision (Centre for Policy on Ageing, London, 1982).

7. Avon Social Services Department, Home Help Assessments (Avon County Council, Avon, 1976). Social Services Department, Harringey, Home Help Allocation Study (London Borough of Harringey, London, 1979). B. Hurley and L. Wolstenholme, Strategy for the Elderly (City of Bradford, 1979). Social Services Department, Hammersmith, Monitoring Home Help Assessments and Allocations (Clearing House for Local Authority Social Services Research, Birmingham University, No. 4, 1974, Birmingham). J. May and A. Witbread, Equal Help for Equal Need? (Warwickshire County Council, Warwickshire, 1977).

8. A. Hunt, The Home Help Service in England and Wales Cmd. 1973, HMSO, 1970.

9. C. Marks, Home Help, Occasional Papers in Social Administration, No. 58 (Bell and Co., London, 1975).

10. Gwynne and Fean, Home Help Service in Cumbria.

11. Ibid., pp.1,2.

12. Gwynedd County Council, A Research Review of the Operation of the Home Help Service in Gwynedd (Gwynedd County Council, 1977).

13. Institute of Home Help Organisers, 'How do we see social workers?', The Newsletter (August 1981), London.

14. C. Rowlings, Social Work with Elderly People (George Allen and Unwin, London, 1981).

15. Goldberg and Connelly, The Effectiveness of Social Care for the Elderly, p.105.

16. Ministry of Health Circular 12/65: Use of Ancillary Help in the Local Authority Nursing Services, 1965.

17. Ministry of Health Circular 32/68, 1968 and Circular 13/72, 1972.

18. L. Hockey, Feeling the Pulse (Queens Institute of District Nursing, London, 1966).

19. OPCS Social Survey Division, Nurses Working in the Community, (HMSO, London, 1982).

20. L. Hockey, Use or Abuse (Queens Institute of District Nursing, London, 1972).

21. Report of the Sub-Committee on the Use of Ancillary Help in the Local Authority Nursing Services, Standing Nursing Advisory Committee, Central Health Services Council, MOH, 1965.

22. MOH Circular 12/65, 1965.

23. Scottish Home and Health Department, Circular SHM 70/1970 and LHAS 10/1971. SHHD, 1970.

24. Scottish Home and Health Department, Circular No. 1977 (Gen) 35, Training and Duties of Nursing Auxiliaries and Nursing Assistants, SHHD, 1977.

25. Ibid., appendix.

26. The Development of Nurse Education, Working Group 3, Consultation Paper 1, United Kingdom Central Council for Nursing Midwifery and Health Visiting. January 1982.

27. OPCS, Nursės Working in the Community.

28. K.R. Poulton, Evaluation on Community Nursing Service of Wandsworth and East Merton Teaching District (Wandsworth and East Merton Health District, London, 1977).

29. M.L. Johnson with S. Di Gregorio and B. Harrison, Ageing, Needs and Nutrition (Policy Studies Institute, London, 1982).

30. J. Burnett, Plenty and Want: A Social History of Diet in England from 1815 to the present Day. (Thomas Nelson, London, 1966).

31. I. Harris, Meals on Wheels for Old People (Government Social Survey, London, 1961) p.4.

32. Johnson, Ageing, Needs and Nutrition, p.10.

33. DHSS Meals Services 1978-79: England, Personal Social Services: Local Authority Statistics (DHSS, London, 1980). IMTA Welfare Services Statistics. R. Wager, Care of the Elderly (EIU Estimates 1971).

34. A. Hunt, The Elderly at Home (HMSO, London, 1978).

35. Johnson, Ageing, Needs and Nutrition.

36. N. Connelly and E. Goldberg, 'Looking at Meals on Wheels', Community Care (14 June 1979) London.

37. DHSS Circular 5/70: Organisation of Meals on Wheels. DHSS, London, 1970.

38. N. Connelly and E. Goldberg, Looking at Meals on Wheels.

39. G. Stanley and W. Lutz, Meals Services for the Elderly in Scotland (Scottish Home and Health Department, 1976).

40. B.R. Stanton, Meals for the Elderly (King Edwards Hospital Fund, London, 1971).

41. M. Meacher, 'The Old, the Future of Community Care', in The Fifth Social Service: Nine Fabian Essays (Fabian Society, London, 1970).

42. Office of Health Economics, Malnutrition in the 1960s (OHE, London, 1967).

43. M. Johnson, Meals Services for Elderly People: An Overview of Three Studies (Policy Studies Institute, London, 1982).

44. DHSS Circular 5/70: Organisation of Meals on Wheels. DHSS, London, 1970.

45. MOH Circular 100/48: National Health Service Act 1946, Part 3: Recovery of Charges under Section 22(2), 28(2). MOH, London, 1948.

46. K. Judge and J. Matthews, Charging for Social Care (National Institute Social Services Library, London, 1980).

47. Hunt, The Home Help Service in England and Wales (HMSO, London, 1970).

48. DHSS Circular 53/71: Help in the Home: Section 13 of the Health Services and Public Health Act 1968, DHSS, London, 1971.

49. E. Ferlie and K. Judge, 'Retrenchment and Rationality in the Personal Social Services', Policy and Politics Vol. 9, No. 3, 1981.

50. Hansard Vol. 986, Col. 835 of 12-6-1980.

51. M. Hyman, The Home Help Service (Redbridge Social Services Department, 1980). See also Home Help Service in Cheshire: Consumer View (Cheshire Social Services Department, 1980).

52. Hunt, The Home Help Service in England and Wales.

53. Home Help Service in Cheshire.

54. Hyman, The Home Help Service.

55. N. Howell, D. Boldy and B. Smith, Allocating the Home Help Service (Bedford Square Press, London, 1979).

56. Surrey County Council, Community Support Scheme for the Elderly (Social Services Department, 1981).

Chapter Five

INNOVATIONS

This chapter is concerned with an analysis of community care innovations aimed at supporting the elderly in their own homes. In particular I want to discuss Hospital at Home schemes and their development in the United Kingdom. New areas of work in the home help services, home nursing services and foster care schemes for the elderly will also be examined. I will also discuss some projects which are in the forefront of the trend to extend the role of domiciliary social services and domiciliary nursing services.

The merits of Home-Care schemes for the elderly have been widely reported.[1] The development of Home-Care schemes in the United Kingdom have been very slow despite their success in the United States, France, Canada and Israel. There is mounting and consistent evidence that many elderly people are placed in institutions such as Old Persons' Homes, Hospitals and Nursing Homes not for medical reasons or because they need nursing care, but because essential community support services are lacking. In one study in Massachusetts it was found that only 37 per cent of 100,000 patients in nursing homes needed skilled nursing care and nearly 50 per cent required only limited and periodic supervision.[2] The inappropriate use of skilled nursing and medical services and the blocking of hospital beds because of this lack of community support or appropriate community service, is both wasteful and costly. It also is a disadvantage to elderly people who might wish to stay in their own homes if the support service were available. In the United States of America in the past 30 years there has been a big increase in the number of Home-Care programmes. In 1955 there were only 20 such schemes, by 1967 this number was over 1,800.[3] The first Home-Care scheme in Israel was set up in 1958 but the first scheme organised as a preventative service for the elderly was only begun in 1970. The criteria for admission to the scheme was the need for in-home services. The basic services are provided by doctors, nurses, social workers and physiotherapists. The home care team assumes full responsibility for the provision of all the services that the patient needs to be nursed and treated at home.[4]

The first discussion on the appropriateness of such a scheme in the United Kingdom was in relation to a service for the elderly in 1950. The initiative for such a programme was a reaction to the blockage of hospital beds by the elderly in geriatric hospitals. Dr E. Brook a physician in charge of a large hospital for the elderly outside London argued for more support for the elderly in their own homes rather than the provision of more and more hospitals. The aim of these support services was to provide the services that the elderly person would have enjoyed in hospital such as diagnostic facilities, treatment facilities, nursing care, social work, meals and laundry services. Dr Brook felt that such a scheme would have saved hospital beds, kept many elderly persons out of hospital, and provided the answer to the nursing and bed shortage.[5] Dr Brook's concept had to wait another thirty years before being taken up. However the basis of the English experiments came not from Dr Brook but from France. In 1980 as in 1950 there was a shortage of hospital beds for the elderly with the consequent build up of waiting lists and inappropriate occupancy of hospital beds by the elderly. Health Authorities, because of these problems, began to look for alternative methods of caring for the elderly.

To understand fully the English projects it is necessary to examine the French schemes upon which they were based. Both the English and French proportion of elderly persons in the population are similar.[6] However, France has 47 hospital beds per 100,000 of the elderly population compared to England where most Health Authorities fall well below the norm set by the Department of Health of 25 beds per 1,000 of the population. Medical expenses incurred by users of the services in France are reimbursed by the Securité Sociale. The employer and employees make contributions to this health insurance scheme in much the same manner as in England. However, in France, unlike England, the patients pay for the services and are reimbursed at least 70 per cent of the cost of medical care. In the case of elderly persons they are reimbursed 100 per cent of the costs of all medical care. Also, unlike England, France has a flourishing private health sector. The private sector is flexible and is able to meet the medical and social needs of patients. General Practitioners, nurses and physiotherapists may also work privately. Local Authorities organise and manage such services as domiciliary health and social care as well as nursing services. As the costs of medical care are reimbursed, patients use either the private or state run medical and social care schemes as they wish. The French private sector cannot be compared with the English private schemes for that reason. Unlike England the private sector not only serves the wealthy or those who are able to contribute to insurance schemes but also the poor. Home-Care schemes vary from area to area but some major elements of all schemes are; "That each service is an independent entity: that each has to sign a contract with the social security administration in which are laid down conditions which the service has to meet for minimum quality of care for admission and for costs (otherwise patients using it would not be reimbursed - the role of the social security is thus powerful in determining a variety of policies); that admission to the scheme is generally dependent upon the patient having been in hospital immediately before being admitted to the Home-Care scheme; and that the scheme is staffed by medical social workers and by trained nurses who supervise Caring Aides (something between a nursing auxiliary and a home help) who are qualified and are also employed in hospitals. Medical responsibility is carried by the G.P. working in consultation with the hospital consultant where necessary? One such Home-Care scheme provides a twenty-four hour a day nursing service for patients who have not been admitted to or discharged from hospital. The Santé Service-Baynonne scheme upon which the English schemes are based is available to those who have been in hospital and those who do not wish to avail of admission but want to be treated in their own home. The scheme is above all a service to the elderly. "The basic aims of Santé Service-Baynonne are: a) to co-ordinate the possibilities of treatment which already exist; b) to put at the disposal of the patient and Doctor the essential personnel to ensure adequate supervision and care; c) to provide essential materials to improve the comfort of the patient".[8] These services allow the elderly person to stay in their own home and receive the treatment and nursing care that they would receive if admitted to hospital. The service provided is very comprehensive, equipment such as special beds, wheel chairs, oxygen and equipment for various treatments is available to the client. Treatment is supervised by qualified nurses. Because of the problem of too few qualified nurses, caring aides (Aides-Soignants) are recruited and trained to carry out basic nursing duties and domestic tasks. They combine the usual duties of auxiliary nurse and home help and are allocated to patients living in their own locality. The scheme employs a Headquarter Staff, Social Workers, Nursing Supervisors, Nurse Caring Aides and Home Helps.[9] The advantages of the schemes are numerous. The elderly patient has a sense of security, being looked after in his own home in familiar surroundings. Being nursed at home allows the elderly person's relatives and friends to contribute to the care of the patient and also makes it possible for the old person's spouse or relative to carry on working in the knowledge that the elderly person is in the care of qualified persons. The whole treatment programme is individualised to meet the needs of each patient. It has also been found that the costs of the service are considerably cheaper than hospitalisation. In the Basque Country it was found to be 42 per cent less and in Paris 33 per cent cheaper.[10]

The attempts to introduce Hospital at Home schemes in this country have been based on the French system.[11] Most of the English schemes apply the following criteria for the admission of patients to the scheme.

1. If there was no scheme, the patient's condition would necessitate admission to hospital.
2. The patient and those who live with them or their relatives must agree to treatment at home.
3. The patient's condition must be such that treatment can be administered safely at home.
4. The home environment must facilitate and be suitable for the treatment of the patient's condition.
5. The patient must be able to recover quickly or at least find illness at home less distressing than treatment in hospital.

The most serious attempt to implement the lessons learned from overseas was carried out by the

Peterborough Health District in the late 1970s.

For years the British National Health Service has tried to set up schemes to nurse patients at home particularly elderly persons. The tripartate structure of the service and the split in the delivery of domiciliary services between health and social services has militated against this concept of care in the home as did lack of communication between personnel in different professions helping the elderly. It has been the experience in the French schemes that experiments were not able to expand into successful programmes if there was a lack of home aides or home helps.[12] The cost of and shortage of hospital beds and the consequent build up of waiting lists with the knock on effect on the social services, domiciliary care services, and domiciliary medical and nursing services led Peterborough Health District to examine other methods of treating ill persons. Peterborough Health District has always had to operate with stretched health facilities as the provision of services in the District has always fallen far short of demand. Peterborough's existing health and hospital services were planned in the 1950s to meet the needs of a small town and its environs. Peterborough was designated a new town development area in 1967 with a population of 81,000 which has now grown to over 113,000. The number of hospital beds for geriatric patients is well below the expected norms and the District has also the lowest ratio of acute hospital beds per 1,000 of the population in the East Anglia Region.[13] It was against this background of shortage of facilities and an expanding population that the Authority decided to experiment with the operation of a Hospital at Home scheme. The scheme was initially set up with three qualified nurses, eight whole time equivalent home aides and one social worker. The home or patients aides were modeled on the 'aides' in France and recruited from mature women living in the locality who had some experience of looking after the sick. They received some training to enable them to function more effectively. The duties of this post were those of a cross between a home help and community nursing auxiliary. They provided a spectrum of care, from bathing a patient to the provision of a domestic service, and advising the patient and relatives on the care of the patient. Clinical responsibility for the treatment and supervision of the patient was in the General Practitioner's hands.

The French Authorities had found difficulty in

getting the Hospital at Home concept accepted by professionals, particularly doctors and nurses who felt that their independence both professional and financial was threatened.[14] Many of these problems were encountered in the Peterborough scheme and were put forward as reasons for the failure of the first scheme. The professional jealousies of nurses who did not wish their patients looked after by unknown nurses, and the lack of involvement of the domiciliary medical services such as the General Practitioner and district nurse, all contributed to the lack of success of the scheme.[15] Lessons were learned by those responsible from the first attempt and a new scheme was set up under the management and supervision of the Community Nursing Service. The new project comprises a "bank of qualified nurses, state enrolled nurses and patient aides. There is secretarial help and a part time social worker, physiotherapist and occupational therapist. When a patient is admitted to the scheme the attached district nurse is primarily concerned. When needed she may call on bank nurses to help with the patient for Hospital at Home care or with her other work. If necessary 24 hour cover can be given to a patient, but in practice the average cover is, for each patient daily, sister in charge (0.84 hours), bank SRN (1.36 hours), bank SEN (1.86 hours), patients aide (5.00 hours)".[16] The scheme caters for about eight patients at any one time. The patients are visualised as fitting into one of the following categories or groups. Those with "high needs" who require care for up to 16 hours a day, those with "moderate needs" and those with "low needs" who only need care for four or five hours a day. The average age of the persons helped by the scheme was 71 years with the oldest being 95 years of age. The most common tasks undertaken by the qualified nurse, was supervision of patients aides, nursing procedure and support and supervision of the patient. The patient aides undertook such work as bathing the patient, basic nursing, provision of meals, bed making and help with personal tasks.

The costs of the scheme were compared to other options the patient could have exercised. The results show that the Hospital at Home scheme proved more expensive per case but the patient spent less time receiving the service than in most schemes. The patient spent on average 16.76 days supported by the service at a cost per day of £43.05 per day. A total cost per patient of £721.61. The costs for patients admitted to a General Practitioner Unit for 31.8 days was £30.32 per day, a total cost of £962.97 per case. Patients admitted to a mainly acute unit spent on average 9.7 days receiving support at a cost of £49.12 per day. A total cost per patient of £475.92. Costing of this scheme did not include expenditure on medical salaries or medication. The costing of the other schemes, therefore, excluded these costs. The scheme has now been adopted by the Health Authority and budget provision made for future years.

The scheme and similar ones have many advantages for the Authorities and patients alike. A standard of care is offered equal to that provided in hospital and the psychological benefit to the patient of being looked after in their own homes and with relatives and friends around them is an added bonus to the doctor treating the patient. The important benefit of the patient being able to make their own choice whether to be treated in hospital or at home is obvious. The relief that relatives and friends receive both psychologically and practically is enormous. The patient's spouse or relatives can live as normal a life as possible and still contribute to the care of the patient. It is difficult to see any disadvantages of Home Care or Hospital at Home schemes from the patients point of view provided only appropriate patients are offered the choice and the patients life is not put in danger because of lack of or unavailability of specialist equipment or staff.

To implement the scheme on a large scale would need a change in the attitutde of many professionals as well as changes in working methods and responsibilities. The overlap area between nursing auxiliaries or patient aides and Local Authority Domiciliary Services would need to be examined, and new systems and methods of co-operation and working patterns adopted, if confusion and costs were to be kept to a minimum. The attempts by Home Care or Hospital at Home schemes to differentiate between specialised nursing duties which are the responsibility of qualified nurses and the basic nursing tasks which can be done by unqualified workers is a start in this direction but "the basic work of caring for the sick has acquired the status of less important, menial work, unfit for true professionals and something of an embarrassment, therefore, to an aspiring profession".[17] Someone has to carry out this work for the patient but it is a duplication to spawn a new type of worker when the domiciliary home help has done these jobs in the past. Research by the author which is in the preliminary stages is beginning to point to the fact that there is very little, if any, difference between the work of some home helps and community nursing auxiliaries. Many Health and Local Social Service Authorities have commented upon the similarities of the two roles and are hoping to appoint workers who can carry out the tasks needed to meet both social, domestic and basic nursing needs of patients/clients. In one Health and Social Service District the caseload of the nursing auxiliary and home help services overlapped by 50 per cent and in others the overlap was 90 per cent and 25 per cent.[18] The report which highlighted this overlap and duplication however did not recommend the amalgamation of the two groups of workers to form one group, but, surprisingly, recommended that the Authorities define more clearly the tasks of the two groups so that each should only work in his own sphere of responsibility, a retrograde step in my view. The new experiments in caring for the elderly which I have outlined, all pointed to the need for closer co-operation and sometimes for the submerging of identities of various professions in the interests of the patient's well being. All the experimental schemes I examined looked at new ways of helping the elderly in the community but the co-operation and goodwill in the projects seemed, in my view, only to extend to the life of the scheme. As yet few authorities have implemented any experimental scheme as an integral part of their normal services.

One Local Authority has, however, formed a unique team of social workers and what they call 'Care Assistants' who provide assistance to elderly persons living in their own home. Support is offered such as helping the old person to dress, to bath, and help with basic nursing needs. The service is especially useful to elderly persons who live alone, particularly those who are ill and the programme also gives much needed relief to relatives and friends who look after the old person.[19] Many Local Authorities and Health Authorities have supported or co-operated with voluntary agencies in providing domiciliary services for the elderly. The voluntary bodies' ability to react quickly and flexibly to new and emerging needs is seen by statutory bodies as one of the main reasons for supporting and involving voluntary agencies. The Liverpool Health and Social Services Authorities collaborated with Age-Concern Liverpool in 1979 to provide a domiciliary service for elderly mentally ill persons living in their own homes. The project was intended to help alleviate the need for admission of the old person to Local Authority residential care but not hospital care. In this respect it differs from Hospital at Home schemes. The project is financed by a grant under the joint financing scheme and it became operational in 1981 with funding for 48 part-time domiciliary aides who work and provide a seven day a week service. A co-ordinator and clerical assistance was provided and a community nurse seconded from the Health Authority. The total cost of the scheme is £70,000 a year. The day-to-day management of the scheme is in the hands of the co-ordinator. The tasks of the domiciliary caring aides cover such areas as domestic tasks, preparing meals, such work as would normally be carried out by the home help or the nursing auxiliary or neighbourly help. The responsibilities of the aides are as follows:-

"1. To develop a relationship with the elderly person especially by listening to him/her.
2. To use 'reality orientation' with the elderly person if it is appropriate, given the assistance of an induction training course.
3. To prepare and serve meals.
4. Dressing and putting back to bed.
5. Escorting to the toilet.
6. Shopping.
7. Management of money.
8. Laundry, cleaning, housework.
9. Accompany client in making visits outside the home.
10. Safety in the home."[20]

The criteria for admission to the scheme, is that the elderly person must be at least 60 years of age and be suffering from dementia, be living alone or with elderly friends or relatives and be incapable of carrying out the normal household chores and tasks to maintain daily living. The clients are assessed as suitable for the service by the co-ordinator and community nurse and the treatment plan is also decided by them. Most of the referrals for the service come from home help organisers who are already providing a supportive service to the same client. Other schemes have not limited their service to individual groups of elderly clients. Derbyshire County Council in 1976 experimented with a family aide project in the Clay Cross area of the County. The result of the pilot scheme was so heartening that the scheme formed the basis of a County wide project in 1978. Family aides in this scheme differed in their work from the conventional home help in that they offered a more flexible form of personal care and support to the elderly in their own homes. They can be called out at any time of the day or night, work on their own initiative and are capable of functioning in an emergency situation. The service is offered to clients who also continue to receive support from the home help service. Over 80 per cent of the help given by the family aides is home care, 10 per cent is shopping and 10 per cent consists of help with the laundry, night sitting etc. The average age of client supported is 74 with 25 per cent over 80 years of age and many living alone. The types of problems clients had fell into six broad groups. Those clients who received an intense service or domestic help of about three hours a week. On average these clients were over 73 years of age and also received the support of the home help service. A second group were those who received help during a family crisis or illness and a third group were those who needed help to make their homes habitable. Others received a daily visit because they needed help in performing personal tasks or needed checks on their health and others needed support to cope with recent bereavement or illness. These clients were helped to adjust to their new situations and cope with new domestic tasks they had to undertake as a result of the loss of a spouse or close friend. The sixth group to receive help were those suffering from severe handicap.

The services provided in this scheme supported and supplemented the help given by relatives, friends and other services such as home helps and meals on wheels. It did not replace them as in so many other schemes, which might have accounted for its success. The service relieved or reduced the stress on families or those who had to look after the elderly person on a daily basis. The scheme demonstrated the need for less conventional domiciliary services and also the provision of a service which concentrates on the individual needs of clients or families on a short term basis and also in the longer term but with the normal support of conventional services in many cases.[21]

Family aides in other Local Authorities have provided mainly support to young families and have overlapped with other domiciliary services in many cases. One London Authority in 1977 examined this overlap and found some striking results in respect of the home help service and the elderly and the contribution made by social workers to their care. The Authority found that the home help service visited mainly the elderly compared with the family aides who supported young families. Social workers were very rarely involved in cases that were visited by home helps, namely the elderly but they were, however, involved in every case in which a family aide was involved.[22] This work supports other results that the domiciliary services are the main provider of help to the elderly who live in their own homes and that social workers provide very little aid to the elderly.

Many Authorities have tried to involve the elderly themselves in the provision of domiciliary support services. Wakefield District Council introduced in 1978 Caring Aides to help elderly persons in the community. The aides were, however, different from any others in the Country in that they were all recruited from retired elderly persons themselves. Their job was to befriend and provide companionship to socially isolated elderly persons. The aim of the scheme was to help the elderly person live in his own home for as long as possible. The aides were allowed to work 20 hours per week and were paid £16 per week. They also carried out some other tasks such as lighting fires, shopping, writing letters and preparing meals for the clients. The cost of the scheme in 1978 was £5,000 and an enlarged scheme in 1979 cost £25,000. Cheshire County Council has a similar scheme where Neighbourhood Visitors are recruited and work under the management of the home help service. Each visitor is given a caseload of about 20 elderly persons who are at risk or in need of constant supervision to visit and support. The visitor also acts as a link between agencies with specialist help to offer. The visitors who are mainly recruited from home helps, are responsible for providing services in a patch or small area of the neighbourhood and so, as she walks the area, is able to build up relationships with the people and become known to them.[23]

Many Social Service Authorities who have tried to offer new and exciting Community Care initiatives to elderly persons had to constrict or discontinue the service because of public expenditure cuts. Coventry City was a case in point. The Social Services Department in 1976 set up a scheme to try and evaluate the real level of demand for Domiciliary Services in an area of the city and to decide how this demand could be met. The budget of an identified area of the city was doubled for a period of three years for the Domiciliary Services. The extra finance was utilised in a number of ways. The level of home help hours in the designated district was increased to twice the average for the city as a whole. The Organiser recruited to manage the project was placed on a higher salary than other Organisers in the Authority and more clerical support than was usual was given and an assistant was also provided. An allowance of £3,000 per year was allocated to meet incidental costs such as publicity etc.

One of the aims of the project was to improve and extend, where necessary, services to existing and new clients, and/or to extend the service to include other individuals or groups in the community who, although they might benefit from the support of a domiciliary home help, have not usually done so.[24] The allocation of resources and assessment of clients needs was left to the Organiser who had not previously worked in a home help service. She set out to recruit staff without the traditional views and ideas about the home help service. She looked for people who would work unsocial hours and with a potential to do more than just domestic tasks for the clients. The home helps were recruited from those who would, with encouragement, see their role as providing as wide a range of overall care as possible. The evidence put forward as a result of this far sighted policy indicated that a stronger relationship than usual between clients and home helps was established which was made all the more beneficial because the helps were also recruited from the locality, which the clients felt contributed to the development of the working relationship. The Organiser did not have the responsibility for supervision of as many staff as organisers in the rest of the city, her responsibility was about 100 per cent less. She was in fact responsible for the supervision of 20 home helps (12 full time equivalent home helps) compared with 21 F.T.E. in the rest of the city and 23 F.T.E. in England as a whole.

Clients supported by the project tended to receive help for longer periods than those helped in other areas. In 1975 each of the 149 clients received 3.5 hours per week. In 1978 each of the 224 clients received 4 hours per week. Although there was a 94 per cent increase in provision of services, at no time, however, were additional resources given to the project used to the fullest extent.

The project did, however, extend the role of the home help which caused overlap with the role of the community auxiliary nurse. At the end of the three year project the home helps were carrying out more personal tasks for the client. The percentage of client contact/personal care support increased from 6 per cent in 1975 to 19 per cent in 1978 compared with 12 per cent with the rest of the city. These figures can be misleading. The level of care given to clients increased over the length of the project with 12 per cent of clients receiving support on five days a week and 5 per cent receiving help at the weekends. The report of the project written in 1982 did not elaborate on what these personal care tasks were, but from the evidence put forward of the withdrawal of nursing services to the clients in the project it is safe to surmise that many of them were basic nursing tasks. The report argues that the new service provided by the workers in the project were substituting for the community nursing service. The District Nursing Authorities had been able to reduce the amount of services given to these particular clients.

"There was no significant difference in the number of home help clients using the community nursing service, but the level of service to project clients measured in hours per month was less than half that to other clients".[25] The level of service and support given by community nursing auxiliaries was even less, 25 per cent of that received in other parts of the city. The District Nurse supported 18 per cent of home help clients in the project compared with 24 per cent elsewhere in the city. The Nursing Auxiliary 5 per cent as compared to 9 per cent and the Health Visitor 12 per cent as compared to only 8 per cent elsewhere in the city. Over the period of the project the amount of support given to project clients declined with a tendency of the Health Visitors to refer clients to the scheme and when those clients were given a service, for the Health Visitor to withdraw their own service.

This shifting of responsibility and cost raises a number of questions both for the client and agencies which will be discussed later. It was also hoped that the project would provide evidence as to whether it was cheaper to look after clients in the community or in residential care. A preliminary report on the scheme in 1978 pointed out the difficulty of evaluating community care projects of this nature. The report concluded that "personal welfare remained unmeasureable and, indeed, it was revealed how tricky the measurement of apparently simple items can be in practice".[26] The report did however offer a tentative view that the cost of community care in the project area was about equal to the cost of keeping a client in residential care.

Fostering as a form of community support service for the elderly was first reported in England in 1956.[27] Since then there was a slow development of such schemes until the end of the 1970s when they began to be examined by many Local Authorities and voluntary bodies. Social Service Departments today with a progressive care programme for the elderly either provide such foster care programmes themselves or in co-operation with other voluntary agencies. The schemes have been given a variety of names which also highlights the different approaches to their development. Some have been titled adult care schemes, elderly fostering, adult fostering, short term family care placement or foster a granny scheme. Leeds Social Services Department have been operating such a scheme since 1978 which is organised so as to give those who look after elderly persons a short break each year or when a need arises. This scheme relieves, for a short period, the relatives from the very demanding responsibility of looking after the elderly relatives and allows them to have a short holiday or just enjoy a break. The Leeds scheme was not the first scheme in the country as we have seen but it is one of the most comprehensive. At the start of the scheme it only recruited six families to look after the elderly person. The finance originally for the project came from Joint Financing and was in the region of £10,000. The families who offer the fostering service are recruited through advertisements in local papers. This method of recruitment is favoured by many of the departments operating schemes but some prefer to recruit by recommendation or word of mouth as the scheme becomes widely known in the community. The type of persons recruited to the schemes varies. In the Leeds project elderly persons, spinsters, widowers, young couples have all been recruited and consequently the type of accommodation and support offered varies. In 1982 Leeds paid their carers £55.50 per week. The average length of stay of an elderly person in the scheme is between 11 to 14 days but in certain circumstances longer placement is arranged. Priority on the scheme is given to those elderly persons who, without a break, would or might have had to be admitted to hospital care. Elderly persons who suffered from confusion and those who, as their own accommodation is inadequate, would have had to have had a prolonged stay in hospital are also given priority.

One of the drawbacks of the scheme is caused by the attitude of social workers who are reluctant to use the scheme and refer clients for the service. "Social workers are used to reacting to crisis and find it difficult to use a scheme like this correctly, which involves planning ahead".[28] The benefits of such schemes to the elderly are many. Elderly persons do not have to suffer the trauma of admission to residential care and all that such a move implies. The benefits to the authorities of such a scheme are not however so obvious. The Leeds scheme it seemed releases short term places in residential establishments but the cost of the care of an elderly person in the scheme is thought not to be much different than that for residential care.[29] A study of the scheme by Leeds University formed the opinion that the short term placements in foster homes might be cheaper than short term in residential establishments but they also stated that it was important when costing such projects to consider 'hidden costs' of each service before making comparisons. "The result of such comparisons was not as 'favourable' to the family placement scheme as one might have expected".[30]

Summary

An analysis of some of the schemes raises some important questions which must be answered. The Coventry City project also raises some interesting moral and ethical issues. The decision to double the service provision to clients for a set period of time knowing that the support would have to be withdrawn at the end of the project begs the question as to what happened to those clients after the researchers had gone away? The Health Service redeployed a number of its community nursing staff as a result of the extra domiciliary support to clients in the project area. What effect did the withdrawal of Domiciliary Services have on those clients where the nursing service was also withdrawn? Did the nursing service take those clients back on their caseload again at the end of the project? What effect did the project have on the community nursing service in the long term? In schemes such as this, is the main objective of a social service, that is to provide support to clients according to their need, overridden by the short term objectives of the project at the expense of the client and other complementary services? The problems of evaluating community care projects are well documented in Goldberg and Connelly's book Evaulation Research in Community Care.[31] The quality of care provided is particularly difficult to evaluate as was commented upon in the 1978 report on the Coventry project. Evaluation was possibly made more difficult in this project in my view by the appointment of an inexperienced and untrained Organiser. The assessment of clients' social and health care needs is difficult enough when carried out by highly trained and experienced staff. This one fact alone, that the assessment and evaluation of client need and the subsequent treatment plan was supervised by untrained and inexperienced staff makes the whole scheme and its evaluation suspect. Were the appropriate clients selected for services? Was the appropriate amount of support given and for the right amount of time? All these questions are all the more important as the scheme hoped to provide more personal caring skills and support to clients than is normal for Domiciliary Service. The justification, if there is one, for the appointment of an untrained manager to such an important project, which might have changed the future of Domiciliary Services, needs to be spelt out in detail to give credibility to the result of this excellent attempt to provide new Domiciliary Services. Would an untrained social worker have been given responsibility for such a project to measure the effectiveness of social work?

The schemes point to the need for certain groups to examine their attitudes to experimental or new methods of service delivery. The Hospital at Home schemes showed that many an excellent project can be made unworkable by the attitudes to the scheme of nurses and doctors. The attitude of those who work in Social Services Departments, to working with the elderly needs examination if services are to develop. The low priority given to work with the elderly by some social workers is to be deplored. This attitude also means that priority is not given to such services as domiciliary care or meals on wheels, but it is given to those areas that social workers see as tasks needing their professional expertise, such as child care and work with families at the expence of services to the elderly.

While Social Service Staff, Nursing Staff and Residential Care Staff who work with the elderly are moving towards care in the community for the elderly, doctors are spending more and more time in Institutions. In 1948 only 40 per cent of doctors worked in hospitals now the proportion is nearer 60 per cent.[32] A reversal of this trend is needed if effective community care is to become a reality for the elderly. The division of responsibility for client care, particularly the elderly, between the nursing service and the home help service must be clarified if the best use is to be made of resources. The division of the services at present militate against teamwork.

It also raises questions about payment by clients for services. Services provided by the Health Service are free but the cost of Domiciliary Services provided by Local Authorities may have to be met by clients. If services such as community nursing is withdrawn and replaced by a home help service the client may have to pay for all or part of the service. Is this fair on the client who has no choice but to perhaps discontinue the home help service? Whether clients or patients should pay for services is a political decision but the present system is unfair to patients and clients alike who have no choice in the selection of services.

These schemes raise more questions than they answer. One important area highlighted by nearly all the projects is that of the role of the home help and community auxiliary nurse. All of the reports point to the fact that there is considerable confusion and overlap in the tasks that each group carries out, in the minds of both staff and clients. Conflict between the home help and nursing profession dates back to the beginning of this century and was first commented upon in the 1st Report of the Ministry of Health in 1920[33] and has been discussed at regular intervals ever since.[34] Much work needs to be carried out to resolve this confusion and conflict in the best interests of the clients if we are to provide an effective and efficient service to the elderly in the community.

Notes

1. M. Cherkasky, 'The Montefoire Hospital Home Care Program', Am.J. Public Health, 39, p.163 (1959). O.T. Brown, 'Home Care of the Elderly', Practitioner, 200, p.813 (1968). C.F. Ryder, P.G. Stitt and W.F. Elkin, 'Home Health Services - Past Present and Future', Am.J. Public Health 59, p.1720 (1969). H. Kistin and R. Morris, 'Alternatives to

Institutional Care for the Elderly and Disabled', Gerontologist, Vol. 12, Summer, pp.139, 142 (1972). I.G. Mowat and R. Morgan, 'Peterborough Hospital at Home Scheme', B.M.J., Vol. 284 (Feb. 1982), pp.641-643. O.L. Frankfather, M.J. Smith and F.G. Caro, Family Care of the Elderly (Lexington Books, Boston, 1981). See F.G. Caro 'Demonstrating Community-Based Long-Term Care in the United States: an Evaluation Research Perspective', in Evaluating Research in Social Care, M.E. Goldberg and N. Connelly (eds.) (Policy Studies Institute, London, 1981).

2. Kirstin and Morris, 'Alternatives to Institutional Care'.

3. S.A. Wartski and D.S. Green, 'Evaluation in a Home Care Program', Medical Care, Vol. IX, No.4 (1971).

4. G. Librach, C. Davidson and A. Peretz, 'A Community Home-Care Program', J.Am. Geriatrics Society, Vol. XX, No. 16 (1972).

5. 'Home-Hospital', The Medical Officer (26 August 1950), pp.99-100.

6. W.H.O. World Health Statistics, Vital Statistics and Causes of Death (W.H.O., Geneva, 1979).

7. S. Cang and F. Clarke, 'Home Care of the Sick - an Emerging General Analysis Based on Schemes in France', Community Health, Vol. 9, No. 3 (1978), pp.167-178.

8. F. Clarke, 'Home Care - an Alternative to Admission', Health and Social Services Journal (21 February 1976), pp.348-349.

9. Ibid., p.349.

10. F. Clarke, 'Hospital at Home-Patient Choice-The French Connection', Concord, No.8 (Spring 1977), pp.21-25.

11. D. March, 'Hospital at Home', Health and Social Services Journal (1 July 1982), p.803.

12. Clarke, 'Home Care', p.349.

13. A. Hyde, 'A Sense of Adventure', Health and Social Services Journal (25 August 1978), pp.958-960.

14. Clarke, 'Home Care', p.349.

15. I.J. Mowat and R. Morgan, 'Peterborough Hospital at Home Scheme', p.641.

16. Ibid., p.641.

17. S.A. Cang, 'Full-time and Part-time Patients, An Analysis of Patient Needs and their Implications for Domiciliary and Institutional Care', in Jaques (ed.), Health Services (Heinemann, London, 1978).

18. West Berkshire Health District Report of sub-group on Home Help/Nursing Services (West

Berkshire Health District 1980).

19. PSSC, Catalogue of Development in the Care of Old People (Personal Social Service Council, London, 1980), p.7.

20. J.A. Flynn, 'Aides for the Elderly', Health and Social Service Journal (29 April 1982), pp.534-536.

21. A. Barritt, A Family Aide Project in Derbyshire (Derbyshire Social Services Department, Matlock, Derbyshire, 1978).

22. L.B. Wandsworth, Home Helps/Family Aides (Clearing House for L.A. Social Services Research, No. 6, August 1977, University of Birmingham).

23. J. Cheetham, 'Cheshire County Pilot Scheme Neighbourhood Visitors', The Newsletter, Institute of Home Help Organisers (May 1979), London.

24. S. Latto, 'Help Begins at Home', Community Care (12 June 1980), pp.20-21.

25. S. Latto, The Coventry Home Help Project (Coventry City Council, 1982). See also A. Hunt, 'The Home that Jack Built', Community Care (16 February 1977), p.15; S. Latto, 'Help Begins at Home', Community Care (14 April 1980), pp.15-16 and (12 June 1980), pp.20-21; and 'Costs and Benefits of Coventry Home Help Project', One-day workshop-report of proceedings (15 May 1978), Coventry City Council.

26. 'Costs and Benefits'.

27. M. Buck, 'Foster Care for the Elderly', Social Service Quarterly, Vol. XXX, No. 1 (June-August 1956).

28. P. Walker, 'Purgatory or Paradise', Community Care (7 May 1981).

29. Ibid., p.22.

30. Ibid., p.23.

31. Goldberg and Connelly, Evaluating Research in Social Care of the Elderly.

32. See P. Townsend, 'Future Policy Trends: Problems of Implementation and their Resolution; in The Provision of Care for the Elderly. J. Kinnard, J. Brotherston and S. Williamson (eds.) (Churchill Livingstone, London, 1981).

33. 1st Annual Report, Ministry of Health, HMSO, 1920 (Cmd. 923).

34. See J. Campbell, Reports on Public Health and Medical Subjects, Maternal Mortality, HMSO, 1924. Ministry of Health Report of an Investigation into Maternal Mortality, HMSO, 1937 (Cmd. 5422). N. Burr, The Home Help Service (Henry G. Morris, London, 1949). T. Goldberg and N. Connelly, 'Reviewing Services for the Old', Community Care (6 Dec. 1978).

Chapter Six

COMMUNITY SERVICES FOR THE ELDERLY IN SWEDEN AND IRELAND

In this chapter I shall examine the present state of domiciliary services for the elderly in Sweden and Ireland and their development. I shall draw upon the best aspects of both systems and discuss what lessons can be learned and applied in the United Kingdom.

Many of the developmental problems associated with domiciliary services in the United Kingdom have been experienced at earlier stages in other countries and to some extent, have been resolved. The difficulties experienced in recruiting appropriate staff, training, role confusion, bureaucracy, lack of teamwork and difficulties in relationships with other professions, have been dealt with and new systems proposed or operated. In this chapter I hope that by discussing the domiciliary services and their evolution in these two countries that some lessons can be learned and applied in England.

The delivery of domiciliary services in Sweden is the responsibility of Local Authorities in very close co-operation with the medical and nursing services. The split and professional rivalries between services as we know them in the United Kingdom do not exist. The Domiciliary Organiser in Sweden has responsibility, not only for the assessment of client need in the home help field, but also for residential, day care, transport, meals on wheels and other auxiliary services concerned with the support of the elderly in the community. There is much that can be discussed re the differences in the role of the Organiser in the systems of Great Britain and Sweden. The total needs of the elderly in the community are therefore assessed in Sweden by one person, and so, much duplication is avoided. I have chosen to examine the service in Ireland because it is a relatively new service. Many of the lessons learned from England and the European Community countries have been incorporated into the system. There is no split in the delivery of Health, Social Services and Nursing Services. All are provided through one agency the Health Authority. Much also can be learned from the very close co-operation between state and voluntary agencies. The Irish National Council of Social Service now the National Social Service Board is a particularly good example of how volunteers, civil servants and local social service staff can come together at national level to discuss and plan services, and advise the Minister. Most of the local and national social and health service agencies claim to merge their individual interests in the service of the client. An interesting trend in the United Kingdom over the past six to eight years is the call to provide services at a local level to a small neighbourhood. This trend can be compared with the local services provided in Sweden through local welfare centres and in Ireland with the delivery of services at local level through social service centres.

The duties of the home help are more clearly defined in Sweden than in the United Kingdom. Training for Organisers and home helps is a lengthy process. Organisers experience a university training and home helps training can vary from six months to two years depending on their responsibilities. Managers in Sweden are attempting to overcome the problems of low moral and lack of job satisfaction in the domiciliary service associated with lack of supervision by Organisers and lack of opportunity to discuss common problems with colleagues. In order to allow Organisers to spend more time and also to give more job satisfaction to home helps, they have been organised into small teams supporting a group of clients. The home help team allocate their own work and manage their own working day thus allowing the Organiser to spend more time in assessing client need, allocating work and supervising the work of the home help. Many British Local Authorities experience these problems of low moral etc. but only very few are experimenting along Swedish lines.

Both Ireland and Sweden have recently established Government sponsored National Bodies to examine priorities in the care of the elderly. The Irish National Council for the Aged was established in 1981 and the Swedish National Commission on Aging in 1981 also. In both countries new legislation has been proposed or implemented in the Social Service field. On the first of January 1982 a new Social Services Act entered into force in Sweden. This Act was the result of ten years deliberation by the Commission on the Social Services. The new Act brings social welfare legislation into line with changes that had taken place in Swedish society, and new methods which had been developed in the social services. The Act also presents the overriding goals and guidelines for social welfare in its entirety. The social services will be directed to the freeing and developing of the individual and groups of clients own resources. These efforts will be directed to measures which will enable the elderly to live in their own homes and locality. The elderly themselves are also given rights in framing different measures and services.

According to Maddox, a well known writer on the care of the elderly, "Western European countries, particularly the Nordic countries and the Netherlands, have extensive and successful experiences with both Home Health and Home Help Services. The visiting nurse is typically an integral part of the health care delivery system in the countries".[1]

The development of Domiciliary Community Care Services in any country must be closely co-ordinated and developed with other Health and Welfare Services if they are to succeed. Domiciliary Services such as Community Nursing and Home Help Services must be complemented by such services as laundry facilities, clubs, chiropody services and health care teams for the elderly. In Sweden, unlike Ireland, this lack of piece meal development has led to a fully integrated community residential and day care service for the elderly. The absence of this planning and complementary development can lead to unnecessary demands on other services. It should be regarded as a prime or prior task to establish a proper balance between residential and day care and care for the elderly in their own homes. As well as the statutory and voluntary agencies the family must also be regarded as an inevitable element in every well balanced system of care for the elderly. All the research points to the fact that the family is still an indispensible source of hope and support and care for the elderly. Domiciliary care is a programme whose purpose is to give the elderly assistance in order to ensure that they remain as long as possible in their own homes in the community. This is the stated policy of most countries in the European Community and is very definitely the official policy of the United Kingdom, Swedish and

Irish Governments. In Ireland this policy is relatively new and in the U.K. it dates from the 1960s. In Sweden the concept of community care of the elderly is older as it is in some other European Countries.

"In France and Belgium the development of care for the elderly is marked by a shift of emphasis toward extramural services." The underlying principles of the idea of 'keeping the client at home' was favoured according to scientific investigation: The main factor influencing the spread of the idea was the report of the 'Commission d'etude des problems de la vieillesse' published in 1962. This report takes stock of the assistance facilities existing in 1960 and also gives a survey of experts opinions regarding possible forms of care for the elderly: even at that early stage 15 years ago - the necessity of prophylactic and home help action was expressed in their opinions".[2] The concept of community care in Ireland can be traced to an Interdepartmental Committee on The Care of the Aged which reported in 1968.

Such fundamental research and estimates of need are the basic prerequisite for any policies that are intended to be seen as planned. Services for the elderly in Ireland, Sweden and the United Kingdom include the following basic elements: Some form of domestic help services, a home nursing and support services such as laundry, chiropody, meals on wheels, residential and day care all designed to help the elderly person to live in the community.

Such domiciliary services are a substitute in these three countries for the support of the family because either the family is absent, or will not or cannot help. Some policy makers see the services as a substitute for the family, others see the services complementing the care that the family cannot give when their capacity is overstrained.

In the care of the very old, in particular in the United Kingdom, Ireland and Sweden, domiciliary care services intervene as a substitute for the non-existant family care of the elderly. These domiciliary services substitute, particularly in Ireland, for the care not received from families by the over 75 year olds because a high proportion of them are widowed or single.

In Nordic countries the state has developed very sophisticated domiciliary care services. In contrast, the Republic of Ireland has only in the last ten to fifteen years began to organise domiciliary services in co-operation with voluntary organisations.

This partnership between state and volunteer has been highly valued but is beginning to break down because of economic restraints which do not allow statutory agencies to support them as they would wish.

The elderly in Europe make up approximately 13.7 per cent of the population. This figure can differ enormously between countries. Ireland alone has a particularly serious problem of dependency. In 1971 out of a population of 2,978,248 there were 931,152 children between the ages of 0-14 and 329,819 persons over 65 years of age. This was a 6 and 5 per cent increase over the 1961 figures. The structure of the population in the Irish Republic therefore differs from other EEC countries. The proportion of the over 65s in the population was in 1971 11.1 per cent and 0-14 age group comprised 31.3 per cent of the population. This percentage of the younger age group in the EEC as a whole is only 25 per cent. The total dependent population in the Irish Republic is therefore over 42 per cent and when the 1981 census figures are available this figure is expected to be higher. This dependency problem has implications for the funding of welfare services and the manning and design of systems to meet need. Each country's welfare services therefore, have to be seen against a number of variables such as population structure, economic developments, availability of staff and political philosophy about state involvement in the delivery of services.

The percentage of the elderly in the Irish population has been rising but not as fast as the number of elderly in the United Kingdom. In 1901 the average expectation of life in Ireland was 49.3 years for men and 49.6 for women. In 1960 this had risen to 68.13 years for men and 71.86 for women. The percentage of those over 65 years of age has risen from 9.6 per cent in 1936 to over 11 per cent in 1971. Those over 75 have risen from 2.9 per cent to 4.12 per cent in 1966.

The domiciliary services for the elderly in European Countries must also be viewed against the other services available to the elderly such as the right of the elderly and their families to multiple welfare and financial rights and various benefits under social insurance schemes.

In terms of vision and scope the most well developed system of care for the elderly in Europe is in Sweden. Their system is particularly organised to support the aged and allow them to keep their self respect and dignity in the community.

Virtually every need of the elderly person as applied to care in the community is assessed and made available. Meals on Wheels, Hairdressers, Chiropodists, transport services, home help services, day care and residential services and holiday facilities are made available in a planned manner. In both the United Kingdom and Sweden legislation established the requirement of the domiciliary care services. These services must be established in local communities. In Ireland the establishment of domiciliary services is not mandatory upon statutory health and welfare agencies.

Ireland

The early development of services for the poor in Ireland was closely influenced by development in the United Kingdom. Between the date of the beginning of the Irish State in 1922 and 1947 there were very few developments in community care services. In 1947 Central Government Departments were re-organised and a new Department of Health and Social Welfare emerged. New Health Authorities (Local Authorities) managed or supported voluntary organisations in providing domiciliary care services such as Home Nursing, Home Helps, Meals on Wheels and Chiropody services on a very limited basis. Some voluntary organisations specialised in providing one service and others provided services for the elderly as part of a larger system.

The Health Act 1970 established eight regional Health Boards to replace the old Local Health Authorities and local dispensaries. The Health Boards now provide all hospital, community health and social services. In the early 1970s Health Boards funded voluntary agencies, such as care of the aged groups, who employed home helps, chiropodists and social workers. These voluntary organisations also received grant aid towards capital expenditure. As Health Boards developed their own services in the mid 1970s and with the introduction of strict budgetary control, because of the National economic crisis, Health Boards have begun to provide some of the services themselves and correspondingly reduced their financial contributions to voluntary agencies.

The overall management of the Health Boards is in the hands of persons appointed by the Minister of Health, drawn from various professions and political parties. The Board is managed on a day to day basis by a Chief Executive supported by a number of Programme Managers responsible for community care programmes, each of these Programme Managers is supported by Community Care Managers, Social Workers and Nurses. The Eastern Health Board which serves the most populated part of the Country has, for instance, eight community care teams. Supporting the statutory services in this Health Board area are nearly 90 voluntary agencies providing services for the elderly.

The Minister of Health in 1971 set up a National Council of Social Service. This body, in addition to considering problems of the care of the aged, had a much wider brief which also concerned the consideration of wider social problems in the community. This committee was established to stimulate and encourage the formation of local social service committees and then to support these groups.

The Council also provided a National Forum for discussion between these local groups and National statutory and voluntary agencies. The National Council of Social Service was reconstituted in 1975 to allow it to promote co-operation between local and statutory organisations. It was also to provide a uniform service over the Country and allow it to give advice on Social Welfare Policy to the Government and Health Boards.

The Council was again re-organised in 1981 to be known as the National Social Service Board to provide administrative support and services to two new Committees, The National Council for the Aged, and the National Council for Children.

The first major examination of the needs of the elderly in Ireland was carried out by an Inter-Departmental Committee on the Care of the Aged in 1965. This committee reported in 1968.[3] The committee examined all aspects of services for the elderly and amongst its many recommendations was the establishment of a National Council for the Aged along the lines of the English National Old Peoples Welfare Committees set up in 1940. The report also pointed out the lack of community support services for the elderly especially domiciliary services such as home helps, community nurses, chiropody services and laundry services. Despite the fact that health authorities could offer support and financial assistance to anybody providing services to the elderly, these services were very under developed as the 1965 committee found. The Irish National Council for the Aged was established in 1981 to try and remedy this situation and to advise the Minister of Health on all aspects of the welfare of the aged either on its own initiative or at the request of the Minister. The Council is made up of 36 persons appointed by the Minister. The appointees represent both statutory and voluntary agencies providing service to the elderly. The Minister at the inaugural meeting of the Board in 1981, stated that he hoped that the new body would reflect the voice of the aged and of those who were best placed to influence attitudes and policies. Policies on the care of the aged in Ireland, he stated, are based on two premises, that the elderly should be enabled to stay in their own homes for as long as possible, but if they have to enter residential establishments these should clearly be appropriate to their needs.[4]

Very little published research into the needs of the elderly has been carried out in Ireland. The first published research was a small but comprehensive survey of every old persons' needs in the town of Wexford (pop. approx. 12,000) in 1973. This work was commissioned by the local council of Social Services[5] and highlighted the lack of and need for domiciliary services. The second report in 1980 into the needs of the elderly on a National basis again highlighted the lack of community care services for the elderly.[6]

Increasing prosperity, higher marriage rates and greater availability of housing in Ireland in the last twenty years has enabled more young people to obtain a home of their own. This trend has meant that some of the elderly population have been deprived of their traditional family support. It was inevitable that urban redevelopment and increased social and geographical mobility coupled with a fast economic growth would lead to a loosening of family ties and a gradual decrease in family support of the elderly. The decades of the 1960s and early 1970s were one of unprecedented economic growth and rapidly rising economic prosperity in Ireland. During these years the Gross Domestic Product adjusted for price changes increased by nearly one half. The amount of public spending increased by an even faster rate. Expenditure on public services (allowing for price changes) doubled. This period also saw an increase in the amount of welfare benefits made available to those suffering from poverty such as the elderly. During this period the number of elderly people living alone increased as more and more children moved away from home.

In 1980 the predominant reasons why elderly persons lived alone in Ireland were outlined in the National survey of the elderly "Old and Alone". The death of a spouse or the departure of children or siblings was one of the major reasons why elderly persons lived alone.

Table 6.1 Elderly Living Alone - 1960s and 1970s - Ireland and United Kingdom

Ireland			United Kingdom		
Wexford	(1972)	28%	Great Britain	(1965)	20.8%
Cork	(1972)	25%	London (L.B.Lambert	1970)	34%
			Sheffield	(1970)	35%
			Coatbridge Scotland	(1969)	30.8%

Table 6.2 Marital Status of Elderly Living Alone Ireland 1980

Status	Women	Men	Total
Single	30.0%	59.0%	39.0%
Widowed	68.0%	39.0%	60.0%
Divorced/Legally Separated	0%	1.0%	
Not living with spouse	2.0%	2.0%	2.0%

Source: Old and Alone 1980.

Thirty-nine per cent of the elderly in Ireland have never married. People from the rural farming areas are more likely to remain single. Nearly half of the elderly interviewed who lived alone in remote areas of the country have always been single. Widowed people were more likely to be found in urban areas. Over half of the total elderly interviewed were childless. Most of the elderly living alone were in the 70-85 year old range age group. The level of domiciliary service provided fell far short of that needed to meet even existing need.

Table 6.3 shows that 3.9 per cent of the elderly receive Meals on Wheels compared with 2.6 per cent in England. Only 3.3 per cent received home help compared to over 7 per cent in some parts of Great Britain. The Nursing service visited a large percentage of elderly compared with the visiting pattern of Health Visitors and Home Nurses in England and Wales where Health Visitors and Home Nurses worked with 1.5 per cent and 1.0 per cent of the elderly. The nursing service in Ireland plays a larger part in the care of the elderly compared with England and Wales.

Table 6.3 Type of domiciliary help received by elderly Ireland 1972

Agency	Percentage of Help
Public Health Nurse	5.1%
Home Help	3.3%
Meals on Wheels	3.9%
Chiropody	2.3%
Vol. Visitor	2.8%
Religious Visitor	6.0%
Friends	29.9%
Family	36.6%

Source: The Elderly in Wexford 1972 Table 13

In Wexford over 100 per cent increase in the Meals on Wheels service was estimated to be necessary to meet existing needs and a 400 per cent increase needed in the very underdeveloped chiropody service.

By 1980 only 5 per cent of the elderly population were receiving home help and the same percentage received meals on wheels. The nurse visiting service had, however, risen from visiting 5 per cent to visiting 17 per cent of the elderly.

Table 6.4 Services received by Elderly Ireland 1972 and 1980

Service	1972	1980
Home Help	3.3%	5.0%
Meals on Wheels	3.9%	5.0%
Home Nursing	5.0%	17.0%

Source: The Elderly in Wexford 1972
Old and Alone in Ireland 1980

Only one in twenty elderly persons have the services of a home help. Nearly 28 per cent of the elderly in Ireland expect neighbours to look after them when they are ill. Only one in ten of the elderly expected help from the Social Services if ill.

Chiropody was a domiciliary service which the Interdepartmental Committee in 1968 particularly singled out for development. Yet by 1972 only 2.3 per cent of the elderly received the service compared with over 25 per cent in the United Kingdom. Over 25 per cent of those interviewed in Wexford in 1972 indicated that they had some problem with their feet and would have welcomed a visit from a chiropodist. This service is more important, perhaps, for the elderly in Ireland where there are no aids to mobility services for the 13 per cent of the elderly housebound. The chiropody service is therefore essential to help keep them mobile. The Minister of Health planned in 1972 to introduce a scheme to provide grant aid for aids and adaptations for the elderly in their own homes but the plan never materialised.

To help provide a more planned and organised domiciliary service to the elderly the Government introduced legislation empowering Health Boards to provide a domiciliary home help service. They were encouraged by the Minister to make arrangements to provide the service either themselves or through voluntary agencies. This was a continuation of the philosophy of partnership between voluntary and statutory agencies since 1965. In a Health Circular in 1965, the Minister stated - "Voluntary organisations and charitable individuals can be of enormous assistance in the care of the aged and, in addition to nursing, they can frequently arrange more readily than Local Authorities for the provision of services such as home visiting, meals, home helps, social clubs, laundry services, help in shopping etc. Health Authorities should encourage voluntary organisations where possible and should co-operate with them and, where necessary, provide them with financial assistance under section 65 of the Health Act 1953".[7] This advice was re-emphasised again in the report of the Interdepartmental Committee on the Care of the Aged.

The Dublin Committee for the Care of the Aged in 1972 set up a committee to examine the possibility of developing home help services. This committee issued advice and guidelines to both statutory and voluntary agencies wishing to plan domiciliary services for the aged.[8] From very modest beginnings in the early seventies the domiciliary service has slowly grown.

The figures in Table 6.5 are difficult to interpret because the total number of home help hours are not available. It is therefore impossible to determine the amount of help given to clients. A rise in the number of staff does not necessarily mean a rise in the amount of help available to clients as actual home help hours worked could have fallen. There is no relationship between the number of home helps and the total number of home help hours worked.

Table 6.5 Growth of the Home Help Domiciliary Services Ireland

	Caseload		No of Home Helps		Expenditure	Cost per Client
Year	Elderly	Total	F/T	P/T	£.0	£.0
1974	4,675	5,563	97	4,637	627,588	112.81
1975	4,919	5,810	72	4,770	1,132,289	194.88
1976	4,241	5,097	88	3,892	1,114,490	218.65
1977	-	6,021	110	4,554	1,565,000	259.02

The amount spent per head on the elderly has risen by over 100 per cent but much of this would have been accounted for by the high inflation rate in Ireland during that period.

It is well known that the living conditions of the elderly can be a significant factor in allocating domiciliary services. The worse the housing conditions the more support the elderly person is likely to need. This is particularly so for those elderly who live alone. The housing problems of the elderly are considerably worse than anywhere else in Europe. Many elderly people do not even have the basic water and sanitary amenities available to the elderly in other countries.

Table 6.6 Standard Amenities Elderly Households Ireland

	Wexford 1972	Ireland 1980
No basic water supply	3.5%	30%
Inside Toilet	28.0%	
Outside Toilet Only	16.0%	
No Flush Toilet	1.8%	32%

Source: The Elderly in Wexford 1972
Old and Alone in Ireland 1980

In Cork City in the South of Ireland, 10 per cent of elderly people have no indoor water supply compared with 50 per cent of the elderly in rural areas. This poses many problems for the elderly who live alone in these rural areas especially those who are not very mobile. Thirty per cent of the elderly who live in cities have no indoor toilet and 60 per cent of the elderly who live in rural areas have none. This means that heavy commodes have to be moved about the house and emptied and cleaned, a difficult job for the elderly particularly those who are without the basic amenities. These housing conditions of the elderly are a major cause for concern in Ireland.

To try and overcome some of the problems of the elderly in relation to their housing the Department of Health has, in 1982, implemented a scheme to improve the living conditions of the elderly living alone. Finance amounting to one million pounds has been made available to Health Boards to carry out small improvements to the housing of those elderly persons. Under the scheme improvements such as provision of water supply and improvements in sanitation are allowed. The scheme however does not apply to Local Authority Housing. The day to day management of the scheme is organised in each Health Board by a Community Care Task Force comprised of social workers, nurses, welfare officers and individuals from local voluntary organisations who make decisions about which elderly persons will benefit from the arrangement. As well as deciding who will get assistance under the scheme the Task Force arranges to employ persons to carry out the work. This Scheme falls in with the philosophy of successive Irish Governments since 1965 of involving voluntary organisations in the provision of services if appropriate in preference to statutory provision. Since 1965 the Health and Welfare Authorities have been urged by Central Government to make maximum use of volunteers in providing domiciliary services. In specialist fields the main role of the voluntary organisation was to encourage the elderly to make use of the medical services and to draw the attention of the specialist services to the needs of elderly clients. In less specialised fields such as domiciliary services, the voluntary organisations were encouraged to provide the services themselves or in partnership with statutory bodies. The Interdepartmental Committee in 1968 pointed out that voluntary organisations were best placed to provide such services as home helps, home nursing services, finding foster homes for the elderly and the appointment of social workers to train and co-ordinate voluntary effort. Volunteers were particularly best placed to help combat the isolation and loneliness of the elderly living alone. This partnership with statutory agencies has both advantages and disadvantages. These advantages and disadvantages are highlighted during periods of economic restraint and cuts in public spending. Difficulties arise when statutory bodies are unable to or unwilling to finance projects in the voluntary fields as has happened in Ireland since 1978. Since 1978 statutory agencies have been looking at value for money and accountability in relation to services financed by them and provided by voluntary organisations. Many of the difficulties voluntary organisations in Ireland are experiencing at the present time arise from insufficient understanding and appreciation of the respective roles and responsibilities of the voluntary and statutory sector. The voluntary bodies resent the close supervision of the Health Boards who have statutorily to satisfy themselves that a reliable and efficient service is being provided. In the field of domiciliary domestic help services, statutory bodies now supervise voluntary agencies so that they meet minimum requirements as to national insurance, provision of holidays for staff etc. Many professionals in the statutory bodies argue that in some cases workers in the Domiciliary Services are being exploited because those who manage the voluntary agencies allow home helps, who are all women, to work only for 'pin money' and so are very badly paid for their services. Some of the Health Board staff also argue that staff in the voluntary sector have not in the past been interested in clients rights or standards of service. Because the majority of Domiciliary Services are still provided on an agency basis by voluntary bodies most of the staff are not trained to carry out their tasks. Some senior volunteer managers do not see the need for training or development of staff or the need to set up reliable assessment criteria for services. Many put forward that the service, particularly the Domiciliary Services, are undervalued and badly organised because the voluntary sector have not been held accountable to any superior body for provision of the service.

To overcome some of these organisational and philosophical differences, a national conference was organised for all workers in the domiciliary field in 1981. The main aim of the meeting was to try and foster a sense of identity among the workers and discuss policy relevant to the 1980s in the domiciliary field. The conference indentified that most of the Domiciliary Services were provided in areas of lowest need such as urban areas. The highest proportion being in the most populated and prosperous part of the country in and around Dublin City. The Services were managed by unqualified persons or members of other professions such as social workers, public health nurses or administrative staff. Members also pointed out the different levels of service, lack of coherent national policy, lack of assessment criteria and rates of pay for the staff. The rates of pay vary from 50p per hour to £2 per hour. Speakers put forward certain areas that needed further study if the service was to develop to a reasonable standard.

Training for all Staff
Adequate Financing
Review of working conditions and pay
A national study of the Domiciliary Services
Monitoring and vigilance against cuts in the services because of Health Boards responses to Government requests to cut public spending.

Sweden

The size of the small population of Sweden and the country's extensive territory in relation to the size of the population has helped to shape the organisation and the type of Domiciliary Services. The country is sparsely populated and distances are vary large especially in the north of the country. These environmental circumstances create certain organisational and management problems unlike those experienced in other central and western European Countries where there are densely populated areas. On the other hand Sweden has never had to experience the terrible situation created by slum housing with the associated health and social problems suffered by some of the population of Great Britain and Ireland.

The Domiciliary Services in Sweden are usually provided by Local Authorities. The client pays for the service if required to do so. Training for Domiciliary Organisers began in the 1920s in The University of Uppsala. This University turned out trained Domiciliary Organisers and developed a care scheme with the co-operation of voluntary organisations, political and social organisations and Local Authorities. Unlike Great Britain and Ireland the role of the various groups providing domiciliary services are very clear. The training offered by the University differentiated between the various professions. It was taken for granted in 1923 that the work of the Domiciliary Home Help was distinct from that of the Community Nurse. Like the Community Nurse, Home Helps were permanently employed, enjoyed paid holidays and other social benefits.[9] These conditions of employment are only recent benefits enjoyed in Great Britain and are not yet in operation in Ireland, nor is the role of the Home Help and Nursing Service so distinct they are very blurred and unclear and indeed overlap in some situations.

In 1943 the Swedish Government decided for the first time to grant subsidies to Local Authorities (Communes) and in certain circumstances to private organisations organising domiciliary services.[10] From 1944 the service has grown from a full time staff of 495 to a staff of over 70,000 today. The growth in the number of full time staff in the Home Help Service has been dramatic since 1944. 495 staff in 1944, 987 in 1945, 2,613 in 1950, 3,315 in 1961, 4,000 in 1963 and 6,200 in 1967. The total number of staff in the service in 1980 was 70,000. This increase is a measure of the Swedish Government's determination to implement community care programmes for the elderly appropriate to their needs.[11]

The policy of the Swedish National Board of Health and Welfare since its inception has been to provide elderly persons with help at home so as not to make it necessary for them to enter residential care. Every effort is made to make the elderly person's home suitable for him to live in by the provision of community support systems and aids and adaptations in the home. The purpose of these services coupled with the health and nursing services is to keep the elderly active and in good health. To try and achieve this aim the Government plans the total environment of the elderly which calls for the development of a preventative outlook with regard to services both in the organising of short term and long range measures.

To meet its objectives of preventative community care the Government, with its responsibility for a large geographical area and small population has developed a decentralised social and medical organisation operating at local level. In some authorities the Domiciliary Home Help Service is operated by a Home Help Board, in others by a voluntary organisation. Local Authorities have also the responsibility of co-ordinating the domiciliary services and the community nursing service. The provision of the medical and nursing services is the responsibility of the County Councils but they usually delegate these powers to the Local Authorities who provide the services. This arrangement allows for closer co-operation and co-ordination of medical, nursing and domiciliary services. Medical care is delivered through Social Welfare Centres which are combined institutions for the provision of out-patient medical and social care. The Centres provide medical, nursing and social care to populations of between 15,000 to 35,000 people. In the larger populated or rural areas there are also sub-centres which provide basic services only, such as Home Help and Nursing Services. The advantages of such a decentralised system are obvious. The staff make contact and establish relationships with the local population in their own community, and so a sound body of knowledge of local needs and resources can be built up and utilised. The local staff also play a central role in the feedback of such information to the managers of the services which is then usually used in the regular review and development of future plans.

This system of locally provided services allows the staff to spend as much time as possible carrying out the duties they were trained for. The emphasis is on a lack of bureaucracy which allows staff more time in direct contact with clients. It has been noted on a number of occasions that British nurses, social workers, home helps and domiciliary care organisers spend a considerable part of their time in administrative and other duties which keep them away from direct contact with clients. The Domiciliary Services are seen as an integral part of this comprehensive community care system for the elderly. Old people who would otherwise be placed in residential care have, by the provision of domiciliary home help, supported by a regular meals service, occupational therapy and transport systems, the ability and right to keep and live a normal life as possible in their own home. If old people have to be admitted to residential care or hospital their home is always made safe for their discharge and appropriately fitted out on their return home. The Domiciliary Service, in order to provide a comprehensive service to the elderly is planned in co-operation with chiropody, hairdressing, bath services, meals on wheels, occupational therapy and medical services. Because apartments are relatively small in Sweden and, like Ireland, because of migration to cities and the increase in the employment of married women, the responsibility and the burden of looking after the elderly is falling more and more on the State. To cope with this problem, since 1950 a special type of domiciliary home help service has been developed to help the elderly. The service is provided by middle aged persons working part-time. These special domiciliary helps are sometimes called 'Good Samaritans'.

The number of elderly persons receiving domiciliary services has risen at a fast rate. In 1954, 18,325 received support, by 1977 this had risen to over 341,000. In 1980 about 307,000 old people received the service, which amounted to over 44 million working hours.

In the early days of the development of the Domiciliary Home Care Service it was unfortunately presented as a kind of universal help to replace all other forms of community help. In the early 1950s policy makers and members of the service were asking if this undue emphasis on the Home Help Service was drawing attention away from the need to improve the standard of care in residential establishments and other sectors of the service. Many authorities experienced problems of recruitment of suitable domiciliary staff, particularly those authorities which served rural areas. About 30 per cent of authorities had this difficulty but, despite these setbacks, the community and residential care services continued to grow. In 1954 domiciliary help was provided for about twenty-three and a half thousand elderly people, this had grown to seventy-five thousand in 1977 which was over 20 per cent of the elderly population.[12]

The basic underlying principal of care for the elderly today in Sweden is therefore to provide elderly people with a secure economic basis and special care in the community if needed, as a priority with open access to community housing and residential schemes. The following could be said to be the guiding principals of Swedish social policy for the elderly:

Normalisation - to live and function normally for as long as possible.
Viewing the person as a whole - assessing the psychological, physical and social welfare needs of a person in the same environment and context.
Self-determination - allowing individuals to

determine their own lives and make their own decisions.

Influence and participation - that (elderly) individuals should be able to influence not only their own environment but also society as a whole.

Properly managed activation - implying meaningful tasks carried in close partnership with other people in a normal stimulating environment.

The main strength of the Swedish care system for the elderly is the excellent co-ordination of the services, assessment proceedures and diversity of services to support the elderly person. By the middle of the 1970s the Domiciliary Home Help Service was the mainstay and most important community service for those elderly in need. It provided over 90 per cent of its resources to the elderly. This growth and importance of the Home Help Service was due to a number of factors such as the increasing number of elderly persons and the increasing number of old people over 75 years of age. Fewer children born per family and the increased tendency for women to be employed, all contributed to the shift towards the need for the state to provide community support for the elderly. The Domiciliary Home Help Service was able to meet demand because of the availability of finance and staff. The 1980s have brought a change "changes in current social values, shortage of both personnel and money have forced municipalities to reconsider their home help service".[13] Difficulties in recruitment were largely due to the working conditions and the low status of the work. Young staff, many of them emigrants from Finland, are not prepared to accept the loneliness of working alone in the community with little support from Domiciliary Supervisors or without any facilities for recreation or rests in the company of other workers. All these problems are reminiscent of the problems found by the numerous committees set up in Great Britain in the first half of this century to examine the state of Domestic Service.[14] To meet this situation the Swedish Board of Health and Welfare initiated a review and development programme throughout the country in 1979 with the aim of establishing new organisational structures to help overcome these difficulties. Different levels of administration between local and county are being organised to help plan services and attempts are being made to improve the delivery of the service and the working conditions of the community care staff. All these changes mean that workers in the

Domiciliary Services are encouraged to help the elderly to help themselves more than in the past. It has been found in both Great Britain and Ireland that Domiciliary Services Staff both nursing and lay have tended to take over the responsibility for work from the old person instead of attempting to utilise and develop the elderly persons' capacity to help themselves and do things for themselves with the minimum support from statutory services.

The Social Welfare Board in the Local Authority (Municipality) is usually responsible for the administration of the Domiciliary Help Services. County Councils are responsible for medical and nursing services. In the new systems of domiciliary care 35 per cent of the gross costs are met by the Central Government. Eighty-eight per cent of the elderly still live in their own homes. This stresses both the financial and recruitment resources of the Local Authorities. The increase in the elderly population expected in the next 10 to 20 years will place on the Authorities the need to develop more imaginative systems of delivering community care to the elderly in need.

The service organisation to the Nacka region of Stockholm is a typical administration. The office serves a population of 57,000. To meet the social welfare needs of this community in the area of Domiciliary Services there is a transport service for the elderly and disabled, a food distribution service for all pensioners organised on a cooperative basis, a service whereby home helps for the disabled telephone elderly people every morning, eight chiropodists, 12 home help teams with 7-12 members organised by an Inspector, an instructor for the blind, an information service for the elderly, service flats for the elderly and a hairdressing service plus an activity and hobby programme for the elderly.

The whole community care system for the elderly is based entirely on assessed need which is analysed in great detail. Service flats for the elderly are a central platform in the support system and are situated near centres of population, shops, transport systems and other community facilities used by the elderly and Local Community.

The principals behind these service flats schemes are simple and logical. Each block of flats or flatlets must be planned for and around the people who will live in them. The needs of the elderly residents are paramount in the planning of the system. Such things as access, transport, shops and sports activities are all taken into account so that the buildings are an integral part of the neighbourhood. Because of the problems caused by the building of large schemes, in the future the Government will only build schemes consisting of 70 flats or less. This policy was agreed after exhaustive consultation with clients and Local Authorities and communities. Each flat has the usual amenities such as bedroom, kitchen, living area, but they are all designed with the elderly in mind. Each flat has also an alarm system which is monitored at a central point manned twenty-four hours a day. The ground floor and basement are usually used for such things as medical surgeries, chiropody clinics, hairdressing salons, shops, and leisure or educational activities. Other facilities such as workshops and concert halls are provided. There is usually also a cafeteria, a large self-service restaurant which is also used by elderly persons in the community. This catering facility also organises the local meals on wheels service. Meals on wheels services are organised on a three day a week basis. Enough food for two or three days is delivered in special foil containers which means that the elderly person or the home help can re-heat on the day the food is needed. The menus are planned by dietician/nutritionists and the elderly can select from the menu.

In some areas new systems are being tried to help integrate the community and the elderly persons who live in the flats. Nurseries are being attached to the schemes where it is hoped that the elderly residents and children will mix freely.

The basements of these schemes are used in a variety of ways. These vary from laundry facilities, home help offices, therapy pools, bowling alleys, sports and leisure complexes. The local community and residents are encouraged to use these facilities jointly.

The residents are encouraged to bring their own furniture when they take up residence. To support residents the ordinary community domiciliary support services such as home helps, nursing etc., are available to them.

Chiropodists are trained to the minimum level needed to provide the elderly with a basic and reasonable service. They are trained to look after the everyday foot care needs of the old person. The training is not as comprehensive as that given in the rest of Europe. The service is available to all elderly persons either by appointment at a clinic or medical centre or the service is made available in the clients own home. All these services are managed by the Domiciliary Home Help Organiser. She is responsible for the assessment and provision of such services as home helps, chiropodists, meals on wheels, admission to elderly persons accommodation. All the following services are usually incorporated into the home help organisation.

<u>Individual Services</u>	<u>Collective Services</u>
Service available to clients home	Services available at Day Centres etc.
Home Help	Chiropody
Laundry Service	Hairdressing
Meals on Wheels	Library
Chiropody	Study Groups
Physical Exercise	Bathing Service
Transport[15]	Hobby activities
Information on Technical Aids	Restaurant/Cafeteria
Activation	Physical exercises
Rural Postal Services	Physiotherapy
Cleaning Service	Theatre/films/music
Hairdressing	
Telephone Service	
Mobile Library	
Snow clearing	

There is therefore, one overall Domiciliary Home Care Service and by offering all of the above or combinations of them, services can be tailored to individual client need.[16]

The Domiciliary Care Organiser who is responsible for the management of these facilities is a member of the Social Work Department and in particular the section which deals with services for the elderly. Domiciliary Care Organisers are expected to have a high level of education plus two and a half years full time special education and training.

In some areas the Domiciliary Organiser manages the 'service flats' which are the equivalent of the British Old Persons Homes and Irish County Homes. These are residences for the more frail elderly. Being responsible for the management of such a wide and comprehensive service for the elderly, the Domiciliary Care Organiser is in the best position to assess the elderly clients needs in the community and can allocate services without having to refer the client to other sections of the department or departments as is the case in the United Kingdom and Ireland. The Organiser is in a position to meet all the community needs of the elderly except nursing and medical needs.

Because of the difficulties of recruitment of home help staff and the problems associated with the wide responsibilities of the Domiciliary Care Organiser the Swedish Board of Health and Welfare are experimenting with a new system. This new method of organising home helps is termed 'teamwork'.[17] Home helps taking part in this experiment work in groups of 6-15 persons. Each group nominates a leader who is then confirmed in that post by the organiser and is paid a small sum more than the other members of the team. The leader is responsible for the day to day running of the team and the allocation of work. The team works a shift system so that there is a twenty-four hour cover for the client. This system leaves the Organiser time to carry out assessment of client need, review services and support the home helps in the workplace. When planning these teams the local problems and the local environment are taken into account so that a different system may operate in a rural area from a densely populated one. These new schemes have been instrumental in raising standards of care and raising the recruitment of suitable staff. They are very flexible and allow local needs to determine the level and kind of service given. The service can respond very quickly to new needs and staff are encouraged to use their own initiative, something frowned upon in the Irish and United Kingdom Home Help Services.

Table 6.7 Location of dwellings. Elderly. Ireland

Location	Percentage
Centre City/Town	17
Suburb City/Town	36
Village	14
Open Countryside	33

Source: Old and Alone in Ireland 1980.

The divide between town and rural area in terms of where the elderly live is approximately 50 per cent (see Table 6.7) in Ireland yet most of the Domiciliary Services are provided in urban areas, the largest service being in the Eastern Health Board area which is an urban area with the Capital City within its boundaries.

The Domiciliary Home Help in Great Britain and Ireland is expected to carry out many of the same tasks and duties "we expect home helps to do whatever is needed. They are sent in to help. This means unlimited service except for those tasks which cannot be safely undertaken. It is better to give unlimited service".[18] Research in England and Wales has shown that Domiciliary Care Staff and Domiciliary Nursing Staff overlap in their duties. This grey area of overlap is causing concern to social service and nurse planners and managers. Research being carried out by the author at present is designed to identify this grey area and propose new systems to help cut this wasteful overlap to a minimum.[19] In Sweden however duties are more clearly defined. Planners have been aware of the need to have clearly defined duties for Domiciliary staff since the beginning of the service. The duties of the home help can vary from Authority to Authority in Great Britain but in Sweden the service is more standardised and the trained Domiciliary Help is expected "to work in homes of the most varying standards and economic resources and to take over all the regular household duties such as cooking, shopping, cleaning.... and at times doing nursing. The Home Help to old people living in sparsely populated regions where modern equipment is rare..... need help to draw water, fetch wood and shovel away snow".[20]

The difficulties of recruitment and the economic situation in each of the three Countries has influenced the type of persons employed in the service. Sweden accepts young people for training as Domiciliary staff, between the ages of 20-30 years. Great Britain and Ireland on the other hand recruit only mature persons, mostly women. Unlike Sweden, staff in the other two Countries receive very little training nor do managers believe that helps need training. In these two Countries it is hoped that the mature housewife is already experienced in housework and also capable of providing a basic service to the elderly population.

The strength of the Swedish system of Domiciliary Services for the elderly lies in the part played by special housing for those in need of it, the wide variety of services and the important fact that there is one person, the Domiciliary Organiser, responsible for co-ordinating and assessing clients for these services. In Great Britain and Ireland the Domiciliary Organiser is one of many persons responsible for providing a divided and unco-ordinated service to the elderly. The clients and local community play only a small part if any in the planning of services in Ireland and Great Britain.

The provision of services by different agencies at different levels of Government or different geographical areas is one of the major weaknesses in the provision of a planned and co-ordinated service to the elderly in these Countries.

If those of us in the United Kingdom who are concerned with the care of the elderly agree that "the needs and condition of older persons are multifaceted, housing needs are linked to health status and condition and both, in turn, may be directly related to income level. Service intervention, therefore, needs linkages between medical, health, social, environmental, and at times the legal services. One of the primary barriers to the effective provision of services to the old person is all too often the lack of organisational approach to bringing together medical, health and social systems on a co-ordinated and at times integrated approach to the needs of the older individual and family"[21] then we must press for a more co-ordinated approach to services for the elderly. To do this we should take cognizance of what other countries like Sweden and Ireland have to offer. Ireland with its unified medical and social welfare system under one manager and Sweden with its co-ordinated and unified approach to the care of the elderly. Taking into account the best aspects of the Irish and Swedish domiciliary care systems, I hope in Chapter 8 to put forward suggestions as to an alternative service delivery system.

<u>Summary</u>

In the three systems examined in this book, both medical and social welfare services are provided in part by public bodies, private bodies and the voluntary sector. The extent to which one or the other agency or organisation dominates or contributes to the market relates to the political philosophies and the structure and economics of the three societies. In Great Britain the main emphasis is on state provision for all, whereas in Ireland there is a partnership between state and voluntary provision. In Sweden there is state provision for all the elderly but the place of the Local Community in the planning and provision of services is emphasised more than in either of the other two countries. In all three Countries there has been, in the past, attempts to decentralise to regions and small Local Authorities responsibility for provision of various medical and social services. In 1982 reorganisation of the National Health Service is an example of the latest attempt by the Government in England and Wales to allow small district Health Authorities to provide medical and nursing services. As far back as 1954 the Swedish National Board of Health along with Local Government decided to re-organise the Personal Health Services into small units. Ireland began to examine this concept of localised services by reorganising the Health and Social Services into eight Regional Health Boards in 1972. Both Sweden and Ireland have been a swing in population from rural areas to urban centres. The degree of urbanisation in Sweden has moved from 49 per cent in 1930 to 78 per cent in 1975. Six and a half million people lived in urban areas compared with one point eight million in rural areas. Whereas in 1983 three million lived in urban areas and three point two million in rural areas. This swing brings with it the problem of providing services for the elderly who are usually left to live out their days on small farms or inadequate housing in these isolated rural areas. Each Country as we have seen has developed policies to deal with their own particular problems in different ways.

Notes

1. G.L. Maddox, 'The Unrealised Potential of an Old Idea', in A.N. Exton-Smith and J.G. Evans, (eds.), Care of the Elderly (Van Nos. Reinhold, New York, 1977), p.153.

2. L. Rosenmayr, 'Familiare und auber familiäre Betreuung älterer Menschen-Alternative oder Ergänzung?', In K. Fellinger (Hrsg) Altenhilfe-ain kooperatives Problem (Wein, 1975), p.26.

3. Report of the Interdepartmental Committee, Care of the Aged, 1968. The Stationary Office, Dublin.

4. Relate, National Social Service Council, Vol. 8, No. 10 (July 1981), p.6.

5. L. Clarke, Needs of the Elderly in Wexford (Wexford Community Service Council, 1973). The aim of this research was to identify the social and environmental needs of the elderly in a town of 12,000. Every elderly person over 65 years of age was visited.

6. B. Power, Old and Alone in Ireland (Society of St. Vincent de Paul, Dublin, 1980). This is a national study of the needs of the elderly in Ireland. It examines Home Facilities, Housing Conditions, Social Contacts, Community Services and the attitudes of the elderly to living alone, loneliness and services.

7. Department of Health, Cir. No. 48/65, Care of the Aged, 1965, para. 9.

8. The Implementation of a Home Help Service (Dublin Council for the Aged, Dublin, 1972).

9. The National Board of Health and Welfare, Home Help Services in Sweden 1979 (Stockholm, 1979), p.1.

10. 'Home Aides Services', International Labour Review, Vol. LVI, No. 1 (July 1947, Geneva), p.44.

11. Home Help Services in Sweden, p.4.

12. Ibid., p.7.

13. Ibid., p.2.

14. See: Report of the Womens Advisory Committee on the Domestic Service Problem, Ministry of Reconstruction, Cmd. 67, HMSO, 1919. Report of the Post-War Organisation of Private Domestic Employment, Ministry of Labour and National Service, Cmd. 6650, HMSO, 1945.

15. An important part of the work of the Domiciliary Organisers is that of helping the elderly person obtain the appropriate transport. Elderly persons may contact the organiser for a pass to be able to utilise taxis for any journey for a fixed payment. Taxi firms submit accounts to the Social Work Department regularly for the provision of this vital service. This is an expensive service, but it does ensure that the housebound elderly are able to make use of community facilities and also visit relatives and friends.

16. Home Help Services in Sweden, p.8.

17. Ibid., p.7.

18. B. Trager, 'Home Help Abroad. A Review of Selected In-home Services in Western European Countries', in Home Help Services for the Ageing around the World (International Federation of Ageing, Washington, 1975), p.9.

19. L. Clarke, PhD. Research, Department of Sociology, Sheffield University.

20. M. Nordstrom, Kungl, Sociolstryrelsen, Stockholm, 'Reasons for Assistance - Task of the Home Help', in Proceedings of the International Congress on Home Help Services (U.S. Department of Health, Education and Welfare, Washington, D.C., publication No. 17, 1972).

21. K.D. Hondrich, 'Menshliche Bedürfnisse Und Soziale' (Steuerung Keinbech, 1975).

Chapter Seven

TRAINING

There is something to be said for those who rely upon life experience as one of the best sources of training, just as there is for those who believe that domiciliary work with the elderly requires the most intense and detailed training which can only be given over a period of years.

Training today to work with the elderly must not be the slave to one theory or one dominant group but must be central to the demands of a changing world and the changing needs of clients. This is the true measure of the quality of training.

If the objectives of domiciliary care for the elderly are to be broadly based, if they are to be delivered in a co-ordinated manner, and if we are to keep the individualist approach to the client that is necessary, then training is essential. It is all the more essential if we expect domiciliary care staff to function as more than domestics or obedient adjuncts of the nursing, medical or social work professions who do not just follow orders but use their own initiative and independent judgement. If we want domiciliary staff to function thus we must test our methods of work and content of training.

Those who manage Domiciliary Services have an obligation to look at the effect of training. Good feelings and natural aptitude or the will and the good sense of staff will not see them through the difficult job they have to do today. In the ever changing world much is demanded of domiciliary care staff. Care and thoughtful evaluation must be focused upon the content of training to help them meet the demands of today's society. Training must also take into account the trend and changes which are occuring in other professions which have an important bearing on the work of domiciliary care.

Many of the professions that domiciliary care staff have to work with such as nursing and social work are tending to delegate many of their traditional tasks. These groups, in their scramble for professional status, are beginning to examine what 'non professional' tasks they can delegate to allow themselves to get on with what they feel is the work of a 'professional'. This is happening today in the nursing and social work professions. Witness the number of different grades of nursing and social work staff. State Registered Nurse, State Enrolled Nurse, Assistant Nurse and Auxiliary Nurse. Social workers now also have a diversity of grades, qualified social worker, social service officer, social work assistant and welfare assistant. Domiciliary care staff have now the opportunity to develop a skill in areas such as working with the elderly based on the needs of the clients not on the need to a rush for professional status at, perhaps, the expense of the client.

Training which prepares staff to react to already existing social needs, must be oriented towards the concept of prevention and rehabilitation. Domiciliary care staff must be trained to be not only carers but also agents of change, detecting social need and social problems. Because of the trend, good or bad, towards professionalisation of the caring professions, every opportunity should be given to all workers to train together to break down the barriers between the different groups in the caring field.

What then do we teach domiciliary care staff? That naturally depends upon the activities we expect them to carry out. The more we teach them the greater the catalogue of roles and tasks which can be asked of them.

With the expansion and emphasis on community care in peoples own homes the more we must realise that domiciliary care staff are in the forefront of the caring services and therefore need training. This is not a desire to train domiciliary care staff as quasi social workers or nurses but to improve the service to the clients.

Only appropriately trained staff can be flexible enough to respond to the ever changing needs of the elderly. On the whole only trained staff can be aware of the need for changes to be able to recognise and respond to the need and cope with the stress of change. Only staff who are aware can help others to come to terms with change.

No organisation or individual has to date

examined the professional training or educational needs of staff in the Domiciliary Services. Attempts have been made to discover the training needs of manual workers[1] such as Home Helps but these attempts, in my view, are very shortsighted. They view the domiciliary care staff as manual workers rather than belonging to a group with a supportive, rehabilitative and caring role in relationship to clients in much the same way as other staff in social work fields. These training programmes only meet some of the very basic needs of staff. No training in caring skills is given to staff in the Domiciliary Services except those in the home help service. In this area only 63 per cent of Local Authorities provide any kind of basic training to home helps and only 40 per cent of domiciliary organisers are professionally trained.[2]

What can training do for persons who are not seen as caring staff or professional colleagues but as manual workers with a limited role to play in client care, yet spend more of their working time in direct work with clients than any other profession in the Social Service Departments? As more and more young persons enter the domiciliary care field they will demand more concern for social justice, more expertise and some form of appropriate training to equip them to deal with the many demands made upon them and enable them to anticipate emerging needs. The role of the domiciliary worker has changed in the last ten years and is now changing at a faster pace than ever before.

Staff are expected to do more than simple domestic tasks or just drive meals on wheels vans.[3] As many as 120 tasks of home helps have been identified, from simple domestic tasks, to counselling clients, basic nursing duties, helping clients to make wills, attending case conferences, motivating clients, taking part in rehabilitative programmes, giving advice, attending tribunals with clients, teaching clients and children[4], all tasks you might expect a social worker to do at some time for clients. Who can do them most effectively?

Social Service Departments have yet to realise that even the most dedicated workers like those who work in the domiciliary services, need training other than they provide at present, a few days or weeks in duration or 'on the job' training. The problem of devising a training scheme for domiciliary service staff is not helped by the diversity of backgrounds and levels of education of staff. It is comparatively easy to arrange training at present on a very superficial level but does it achieve anything? Training and education is more than techniques and courses. What those organising training must do is to try and create a sense of commitment that will impel staff to want to do their job to the best of their ability and to acquire the techniques and knowledge that are necessary to do this rather than impart knowledge about cooking, cleaning etc. The composition of staff and the diversity of jobs makes a uniform pattern of training not only difficult to devise but, in practice, inadvisable. The domiciliary workers are men and women, young and old, skilled and unskilled, ex steelworkers and housewives, full-time workers and those who only work a few hours a week. They represent a varied cross section of society. They are not people who can be patronised nor are they easily fooled or intimidated by popular or trendy theories. They have to be convinced that the training they receive is necessary and in the best interests of the clients.

The major part of the work of domiciliary workers is in providing personal services to clients in their own homes. Training must therefore prepare them for this kind of work giving emphasis to the practical work and caring skills necessary to do the job. This type of training is more than the imparting of information in a systematic and disciplined way. It is also the acquisition of knowledge, attitudes and skills in which the worker uses him/herself as an instrument of self awareness, responsibility and discipline in the service of clients, not a theory or trendy new service delivery system. This cannot be done in a few days, weeks or even years. The idea that someone can be trained once and for all to do a job can no longer be accepted. The objective of education and training must not be the imparting of a great deal of knowledge quickly, paradoxically, time is too short and valuable for this and, in any event, social problems and methods to combat them are changing and developing so fast that knowledge and education become quickly outdated. No one person or organisation has yet produced a document on what exactly is the role of workers in the domiciliary field. Is the worker just a person who delivers a simple service or can they play a part in the treatment and rehabilitation of clients and their families? Perhaps this lack of boundaries is a good thing in that the service can develop to meet clients needs without going into paroxisms of agony before they change working methods to meet client need. Domiciliary workers both manual and organisers are social workers in the true sense of the word. The Barclay Report more or less stated that any person who works in the Field, Residential and Day Care Sections of Social Service Departments is a social worker but it did not comment upon the status of the single largest group of workers in the Social Services, the domiciliary worker. However, it did point out that residential work was part of social work and research by the author is now pointing out that there is very little difference other than the work setting, in most of the tasks of home helps and care assistants in elderly persons homes. So why is one job termed social work and the other not? Do people know what domiciliary staff do? Is most of the work done by field social workers better done by domiciliary service staff? I believe that it could be and perhaps done with more feeling and empathy for the everyday problems of the elderly. I believe that the work and training of domiciliary staff is too important to be left to staff trained in social work methods.

The first ever encouragement given to Authorities to train personnel in the field we now call domiciliary services was in 1914. The local Government board as a result of the distress caused by the first world war suggested that Local Authorities (Local Representative Committees) should recruit and train sick room helps to help housewives who were "temporary indisposed". The workers were to be trained in simple household tasks. The Central Committee on Women's Employment arranged as an experiment the training of a number of such workers with the aid of a grant from the Queens Fund.[6]

By 1919 the Womens Advisory Committee (Min. of Reconstruction) were pointing out that, the fore runner of the present domiciliary service for the elderly, the domestic service, was at that time understaffed, primarily due to the lack of adequate training facilities. As a result the occupation of domestic was mainly carried on by unskilled workers who were unable on the one hand to command satisfactory conditions of employment or on the other to fulfil their tasks efficiently.[7] This situation has not changed very much in relation to the recruitment and employment of staff in domiciliary statutory services to day. Most domiciliary staff who work with the elderly today have little or no training to fit them for the job. The effect of this lack of training can undermine the most carefully laid rehabilitative plans for clients.[8] Malin has found evidence that domiciliary staff felt unqualified for the task expected of them and that lack of training led to a sense of isolation from the other members of the team. Domiciliary staff were over protective to clients and failed to allow clients to reach full independence which retarded the clients progress and seriously delayed the teams treatment goals for the clients. Malin's work throws important light on the lack of understanding in social service departments of the effect of the lack of training for staff who in the past were thought to have little effect on clients rehabilitation.

The Womens Advisory Committee in 1919 pointed out the inadequate training facilities available. Only 10 Domestic Service Schools existed in 1919 and 4 of these taught only cooking. Four were in the now G.L.C. area and the rest situated around the country. The total number of girls in training was only 350.[9] The training recommended by the 1919 committee looked very much like modern day training for domiciliary staff but a lot more thorough and lengthy. The training was to last two years, 42 weeks a year from 9 am to 5 pm each day. Students attended classes on physical education, theory and practice of cookery, laundry work, housewifery, needlework, dressmaking and household mending in the first year. In year two they studied nursery work, laundry work, physiology and hygiene, sanitation in the home, care of infants and practical work under supervision.[10] This training scheme did not help increase the number of girls wishing to take up the work. To find out why people were reluctant to take up the work a committee was appointed to examine the situation.[11] The committee found that the "most important question in connection with the solution of the domestic service problem is that of training".[12] Witnesses who gave evidence to the committee agreed that the work was a highly skilled occupation in which training was essential. This committee recognised what many people in social service departments today do not, that is that domiciliary service work is highly skilled and needs training programmes of the right kind. Very few Social Service Departments have a written selection of criteria for domiciliary staff or training programme other than the most basic kind. Even in 1923 it was recognised that not all women were fitted to the work of helping people. The committee expressed its disagreement with "the tendency manifested in some quarters to consider that all women no matter their age, temperament, experience or domestic situation" are fitted for the work.[13]

We have not learned much since then. Many people still think that home helps, meals on wheels drivers, and other domiciliary workers need little or no training or proper selection for the job.[14] The committee recommended a full time six months course for mature people wishing to take up the work. A grant in lieu of unemployment benefit was to be payable while the student was on the course. Until the outbreak of the second world war the shortage of domestic workers did not make people take notice of the problem. With the problems and distress associated with the war and their effect upon the family and especially the elderly, the problem of support in the home for the sick and frail became an acute problem. The Minister of Labour and National Service instituted in 1944 an inquiry into the Post-War Organisation of Domestic Employment.[15] This report agreed with earlier reports about the importance of training and also pointed out that domestic work involved close personal relationships between worker and client. As a result of the recommendations the National Institute of House-workers was formed in 1946. One of its tasks was to set up and run training schemes for domiciliary service staff who by 1946 were beginning to spend more and more time working with the elderly. The Institute was also to act as an examination body for staff trained up to the Institute's Diploma standard by other bodies such as Local Authorities. This was the first and only attempt by a national body to try and set a national standard of skills for domiciliary workers. The first domiciliary workers to sit the examination were from the City of Oxford home help service in 1947.[16] The Minister of Health, in an effort to raise standards in the domiciliary services, issued guidance (Cir.118 1947) to local authorities on training and brought to their attention the work of the Institute, and that one of its tasks was to offer advice on training. The authority to take most cognisance of this advice was the London County Council.

A large number of domiciliary staff took the diploma examination in 1948.[17,18] Some domiciliary organisers in 1948 saw that training was essential for staff but this was the exception rather than the rule. This training included teaching on home cleaning, laundry work, cooking and clothing repairs, a training not so different from 30 years earlier but not in so much depth. This training was carried out during the work period of the staff and was of 13 weeks duration.[19] By the end of the 1940s a number of domiciliary staff were in receipt of the Institutes diploma which was held in high regard by employers and brought with it extra payment.[20]

In her report on training for social workers Younghusband in 1951 saw domiciliary organisers as a category of social workers and so began the long running battle between domiciliary organisers and social workers for domination over their training which is still today not settled to the detriment of both staff and clients.[21] Younghusband found that very little information was available on the qualifications and background of domiciliary organising staff other than that they had a background of Health Visiting, Midwifery or Domestic Science. Harris in her excellent study of Meals on Wheels services in 1960 did not mention training for staff involved in running the service except to report that organisers stated that helpers needed to be strong and young.[22]

The first attempt at offering some form of training for organisers was in 1948 run by the WVS.[23] The course in Surrey, one of a number ran by the WVS between 1948 and 1950, lasted five days. Contributors included staff from the Ministry of Health and was attended by twenty domiciliary organisers from England and Wales. Mrs Moore-Ede spoke of a training scheme she had run for the staff in the City of Worcester which lasted two weeks and encouraged the domiciliary staff to think of themselves as part of a team helping the client.[24] By 1959 there was still no organised training for domiciliary organisers and very few were professionally qualified.[25] Only 11 per cent had a social science qualification, 14 per cent a nursing qualification and 2 per cent a domestic science qualification. The Younghusband report recognised the difficulty of the role of domiciliary staff but still did not report that training for organisers was necessary, a poor substitute was recommended, the guidance of a social worker in times of stress or difficulty.[26] In view of the fact that the role of the social worker was not very clear or that of the domiciliary organiser, this recommendation can only be seen as an attempt to make the service secondary to social work and the authority of social workers. The committee thought that some form of social work training was necessary for domiciliary organisers.

Some authorities were reluctant to send

organisers for training because of the cost of replacing them during their training. Others did not favour training for home help staff because they thought training might put off uneducated persons from taking the job.[28] Others felt that if home help service staff were trained they might develop attitudes that were restrictive which might lead them to refuse to do certain types of work and so reduce the flexibility of the service or take other jobs.[29] Sumner and Smith reported that "often the general attitude was that home helps and attendants in residential accommodation did not need training" but one authority attached a word of caution on this in relation to the future "so far we have been able to meet the need, but the new type of home help is changing. We started with people who came because they were dedicated to the service but the ones we get now just think of it as a job".[30] Did this mean that dedicated people did not need training? Training had become an integral part of the preparation of domiciliary staff in some health and welfare departments by 1968. The Local Authority 10 year plans had envisaged the need for the expansion of the service. The service, to attain reasonable standards was felt to need new recruitment and training policies.[31] Training was still the exception rather than the rule. This lack of training was effecting the efficiency of the service and often led to a high wastage of staff. Staff were often left to their own devices to carry out their work by trial and error frequently in ignorance of their true function and status.[32] Some Authorities set up their own training centres for domiciliary services staff and used only their own staff to teach on courses they organised. Other Authorities abandoned the training centre concept because of the cost.[33] A review of the Domiciliary Services by the DHSS in 1972[34] showed that training varied in quantity and quality from authority to authority and that some organisers still did not believe there was a need for training.[35] The Institute of Home Help Organisers only offered guidance on training for home helps. No training was given to other domiciliary service staff. For Domiciliary Organisers the Institute of Home Help Organisers devised a training scheme in co-operation with the Training and Education section of the National Association of Local Government Officers which later led to the Diploma of The Institute. This course is now available in at least nine colleges in England and Wales and Scotland.[36] Despite the shortcomings of this qualification some authorities make the possession of it a condition of service.

One example of a progressive training scheme for home helps was that run by the L.B. of Greenwich which in 1965 created two new courses; one for ordinary home helps and one for specialist home helps who worked with problem families. Both courses were full time for one week and covered such subjects as, care of the elderly, children, first aid, cookery, and such topics as Social Security.[37] Upon the setting up of the new Social Service Departments in 1972 training for all staff was given a new impetus with the employment of training specialists in many departments. Despite this introduction of training in 1972, 30 local authorities had no training for domiciliary staff.[38] Some authorities were fearful that training would destroy the traditional 'homely' approach of the domiciliary help.[39]

Concern about national standards led the Local Government Training Board and the Central Council for Training and Education in Social Work (CCETSW) to organise a seminar on training for domiciliary staff. The seminar examined the training needs of organisers and also looked at their needs to see if they overlapped with other staff in the social service field. The need for training had been highlighted by the vast increase in the number of staff and their lack of qualifications. In 1974 only 10.6 per cent of Organisers had the Institute of Home Help Organisers Certificate, 26.2 per cent had other qualifications such as Diplomas or Certificates in Social Studies or Home Economics. Over 58 per cent had no professional qualifications of any kind.

Since the inception of social service departments in 1972 the domiciliary service organiser numbers had increased by nearly 65 per cent.[40] The reorganisation of the services had also led to a rationalisation of domiciliary services under one manager. This increased the problems of training because of the variety of staff and their backgrounds. Such services as home helps, home wardens, specialist home help staff, family aids, night sitters, meals on wheels and old persons 'sitting' services all designed to help persons in their own home became the responsibility of one person to manage.

The case for training was helped by the argument that the service involved some 85,000 staff serving over 550,000 clients at a cost of over £40 million.[41] However, nowhere in the report is mentioned the needs of clients and the relationship of this need to training. The complexity of the job was recognised as was the fact that many senior staff were neglecting important aspects of their job.[42] No evidence was offered to support this statement. At the time the working party was sitting, very little if any research had been carried out into the role of work of staff in the domiciliary services. A working party of such importance should have only made recommendation based on sound research and knowledge of clients needs.

The recommendations of the working party reflected the conflict at the time as to the role of domiciliary care senior staff. Were they social workers or management personnel? This conflict has not yet been resolved. Domiciliary Care Organisers at the time regarded themselves as managers who needed some knowledge of social work and social services but not social work theory. The working party saw the organiser as having some managerial responsibility but the largest part of the job being social work orientated. Organisers at the time felt that CCETSW wished to make the role of the organiser secondary to that of the field social worker and therefore candidates for their new form of training (Certificate in Social Service) which was and still is not a professional qualification in social work. This new form of training was designed for most caring staff in social services except field social workers who were to continue to receive the elite CQSW training. It was felt by some at the time that the recommendations of the working party were a compromise between those who saw the domiciliary care organiser in a supporting role to social workers and those who believed that the organiser was a professional in her own right.

The working party recommended that any award to be given was to be organised and validated by both the Local Government Training Board and CCETSW. This joint approach became unacceptable to CCETSW who later came out into the open with their views when they reconvened the working party to change the recommendation re validation after taking advice from the Department of Health and Social Security. Paragraph 16.05 was changed from:- "The validation and award of the qualification should rest with the organisations with recognised expertise e.g. the CCETSW and the LGTB" to "The validation and award of the qualification will rest with CCETSW, if the Council has the statutory responsibility".[43] From the first of October 1974 CCETSW assumed responsibility for the promotion of professional training in the Day and Domicliary Care Services.[44] Why did CCETSW exclude the Local Government Training Board? The DHSS legal interpretation that the legislation covered domiciliary organisers came as a complete surprise to most members of the working party whose chairman was a legal specialist.[45] This move was interpreted by Domiciliary Care staff as a further bid by the dominant social work lobby to make the service secondary to field social work.[46] This attitude of the social work profession reflected a tendency by them to react defensively to criticism as they have done on a number of occasions since, particularly in cases involving children at risk.

The working party did however make a fairly significant contribution towards the development of domiciliary services. It highlighted the complexity of the services administered by the organisers. The report did in my view emphasise the management content at the expense of the important assessment and interpersonal skills of the job. The domiciliary organiser is an expert in assessment of need and should for that reason by in the front line of the social services for the elderly and be able to call in such expertise as she thinks fit to help the client. Only 3 per cent of domiciliary staff would today contact a social worker if they were anxious about a client.[47]

The Institute of Home Help Organisers however felt that it was important to have a course which would be college based with a nationally recognised award at the end.[48] The Institute officers met representatives from the DHSS in September 1974 to discuss training among other things. The Institute pointed out that any training without a progressive career structure would not attract the right calibre of person to the job.[49] The Institute revised its own two year training course in 1976 and this qualification was recognised by employers in 1978 for promotion purposes.

Members of the Institute also met CCETSW staff in September 1974. Domiciliary staff welcomed the management element of the working party training scheme but rejected the large amount of social work theory proposed. The Domiciliary Organiser they concluded at the meeting must have a qualification parallel and equal to the CQSW and also be flexible enough to allow for movement between related professions.[50]

CCETSW developed its concept of 'new training', which after a number of attempts was titled 'The Certificate in Social Service'. The new form of training was an attempt to introduce "a single multifaceted scheme to cater for a range of workers".[51] Domiciliary organisers are not represented by a professional representative on the CCETSW Council but by a Ministerial appointment. In 1974 the Institute of Home Help Organisers wrote to the DHSS about this but no change has taken place. So CCETSW continue to legislate and support courses for domiciliary staff without the profession having a representative on the Council.

The new form of training began in 1975. The course is organised on a day release basis over 3 years in most cases and a day a week under the supervision of a study supervisor appointed by the employer. In year one the student studies such subjects as social administration, law, social services. In the second year called Standard Unit the student takes one of the following areas of study, the Elderly, Adults, Adolescence and Children. In the third year unit a number of options relevant to the students area of work are examined, such as Law, Training, Management roles and Theories, Practical Management, Assessment, Home Help Service or Social Work. By 1979 approximately 3.5 per cent of students were from the domiciliary field but in 1982 this had fallen to 2.1 per cent.[52]

This qualification, which is not a professional qualification such as the Certificate of Qualification in Social Work, has by some always been regarded as a second rate award in the social service field. The setting up of this type of course did nothing to remove the elitist attitudes of qualified field workers in social service departments. The British Association of Social Workers has always held that Directors of Social Services (not Social Work) should always hold at least a qualification in social work. CSS is neither a stepping stone to a further qualification such as CQSW nor is it a recognised social work qualification.

CCETSWs plans for training by 1975 carried major implications for finance and manpower in the social services. At the request of CCETSW and the Local Authorities Association the DHSS set up a working party to look at the manpower implications for the personal Social Services. This report made frequent mention but very little of relevance about domiciliary staff needs.[53] They did, however, say that CSS and CQSW had both a significant role to play in the training of domiciliary staff.

The Local Government Training Board in 1978 issued training recommendations (Recommendation 22) for manual workers (home helps) in the domiciliary care field.[54] This paper drew up many recommendations re training for manual workers but characteristically the working party did not have one manual worker sitting on it out of its 19 members. The objectives of this working party's recommendation was to

1. Assist local authorities in identifying the training needs of home helps.
2. Recommend appropriate minimum training to be given to all home helps.
3. Give guidance on areas of specialist courses and refresher courses.
4. Give assistance and help with the implementation of training.[55]

This advice has been further modified by the Local Government Training Board in 1982 as a result of the financial restraints on spending in local government. Recommendation 22 was tested[56] by 14 local authorities. As a result new training material was issued in 1982. Manual workers in the social service departments represent approximately 60 per cent of persons employed. Most of these are part-time and female which may account for the lack of training and career prospects. The increasing emphasis on Community Care for the Mentally Ill and Elderly in their own homes has highlighted the need for appropriate training for the workers.

In 1980 the London Director of Social Services and London Borough's Training Committee agreed that training resources were inequitably distributed in favour of staff not in areas of service priority such as caring for the elderly. A working group held a conference in early 1982 to look at the training needs of manual staff. They examined the argument that, as Domiciliary staff did not do 'Social Work tasks', hence they required less training than 'Professional' Staff.[57] No research has to date been carried out to substantiate that statement, there is even still argument today as to what exactly social workers do.[58]

Price, a London Social Services Director, put the argument for training manual staff very succinctly when he said "It is a curious symptom of our social and intellectual elitism that the Social Workers who start off with the lengthy professional training provided at the expense of a state requires continuing training 'on the job' to ensure that his or her innate humanity remains accurately focused: yet the Care Assistant or Home Help, who rarely had any prior training before appointment, may still not be offered anything on an in-service basis once on the job". It is a curious principle of giving more to those who have already had a good deal out of the state's education system. "The facts are boring and unspectacular, but if we are not all so numbed by other besetting problems, they should shame us".[59]

Unlike this working party I believe that piecemeal change in the present training programme is not enough. Major changes are needed and a vast redistribution of training resources in favour of non field work manual staff.

At present the training of Domiciliary Staff varies from Country to Country. This variation is a response to the historical development of the services in these countries. Training schemes in some Countries are ambitious, Sweden has a training scheme of two years duration which might not be applicable to the UK because Domiciliary Staff in Sweden perform a broader role in the community than in the UK.

In 1959 the International Council of Home Help Service was founded in Woudschoten in Holland. One of its roles is to publish and promote research in the Domiciliary Services and to promote training. The Council of Europe in 1977 adopted recommendations on the Domiciliary Services in Europe. Part of this resolution concerned training and recommended European Governments to ensure that staff received the following type of training which was seen as a minimum training for the job.

"A basic theoretical and practical training including subjects such as: Training in ordinary domestic tasks, nutrition cooking, dietetics, budget management and consumer education. Health education, hygiene, simple care of children and sick and old people. Training in family and human relationships. Element of health and social organisation professional ethics.
Offer refresher and advanced training facilities in order to enable staff to obtain career advancement."[60]

The United Kingdom has not adopted any of these recommendations. Some Countries have developed their Domiciliary Service for the Elderly to a much greater extent. The attitude in many Countries to Domiciliary Care in the home is expressed in an article about the services in Sweden.

"In my Country we now find it natural for various reasons - humanitarian, labour economic and social economic - that nobody should stay in an Institution if his social or medical problems can be solved in other ways. No old person should live in an Old Age Home just because he has nowhere to live, lacks furniture or cannot clothe, clean or cook for himself."[61]

Most European Countries have very well developed ideas about the qualities or characteristics necessary for staff in the Domiciliary Care Services. In France staff need good health, a capacity for observation, a systematic approach to the job, a sense of organisation, good sense and sound judgement, a capacity to adapt to people with flexibility and understanding and maturity. Recruits also have to take an entrance examination so as to show that the candidate would be able to make the best use of the training. This examination consists of tests in spelling, language formation, aptitude tests and a trial period on the job.[62] Denmark's Domiciliary Care workers should be kind and helpful and always bear in mind that the sick and elderly are often in difficult situations.

Some Countries regulate the age at which workers can be recruited and trained. Sweden has an age regulation that workers must be between 20 and 30 years of age. Recruits are given 15 months or 3 months residential training according to their background and experience. Training is free of charge, the costs being borne by the state. Certain persons such as widows, single parents with dependents can obtain training allowances to cover the costs of the course as well as support for the dependents, rent and clothes.[63] There is a greater emphasis on household services on courses in France and Sweden, whereas in Germany and Finland a greater part of the training is devoted to the care of the sick. However today more and more training in basic nursing skills such as bathing, application of simple dressings is now being given in Sweden.[64]

Courses in the UK rely primarily on 'on the job' training or short training courses in colleges.

Organisers receive two and a half years training in Sweden. Holland has a similar type of training to that in the UK which is two years part-time training at colleges. Holland trains three types of Domiciliary Worker. Home Makers, Home Helps and Helpers for the Elderly. Helpers for the Elderly are usually mature women who receive in-service training to equip them for the job as compared to the Home Makers who are girls over 18 years and have attended a two year full-time course at a recognised Home Help training school. Organisers are trained as Social Workers or as Middle Managers. Organisers must be trained before taking up an appointment.[65]

France in response to its 'Hospital at Home Schemes' has developed Caring Aides (aides-soignantes) who combine the service of Home Help and Nursing Aide. They are recruited from middle aged women who have had the experience of looking after elderly persons. They attend a training course lasting 2 years of one and a half hours a day.

The Irish Republic has one of the newest Domiciliary Care Services for the elderly. In 1972 a working party was set up by Dublin Council for the Aged to advise on the implementation of Domiciliary Services. This working party report argued for very little training.[67] In 1972 legislation was introduced which allowed the Health Boards and Voluntary Organisations to set up Domiciliary schemes with Central Government finance. These schemes now employ about 5,000 staff. There are one or two training schemes but with most Organisers having no training themselves they possibly have difficulty in recognising the need for training in their own staff. One or two Organisers, however, show a very far sighted attitude towards training. Ballymun, an area of Dublin, which has many social problems and a large proportion of its population living in high rise flats, have a home help service which is trained to a high level by Irish standards. The training is a response to the needs of the Domiciliary Care staff in that area.

In 1980 the National Industrial Training Organisation (AnCo) agreed to organise and fund a full-time six week course. Emphasis was placed not only on learning new skills but also on the personal development of the Domiciliary Staff themselves. The training scheme is a conscious effort on the part of the Organiser to improve the effectiveness of the services and also to create a sense of teamwork in the carers. The training in this new Irish service is constantly being assessed and re-designed. Training in leadership skills is also being offered as is training in management and organisation of co-operative self help schemes.

Training and Development: A New Start

At present the various services for the elderly have

their limited individual methods of assessment to determine and measure need. These function most of the time independently of each other. All attempts to determine need, or set priorities, based on present methods of assessing the quality or quantity of the clients circumstances, fail for a number of reasons. They, in most cases, are too restricted to one area of need. They fail to take account of the total needs of the client. Assessment methods must take account of the total person. There is a lack of objective assessment methods in the social services and, in the domiciliary field there, is the danger that each organiser will impose his own idiosyncratic view of need. Much research needs to be carried out in this field. How far could a common assessment method be used in differing parts of the country? Who needs to be part of the assessing team? What information is needed to make an objective assessment of the individual clients' need? Can it be done? Many people argue that the 'intuition' used by many organisers is far superior to assessment aids or priority scalings. Much work is necessary before these questions can be answered. What is certain is that the organiser or one worker cannot, on their own as at present, make an efficient and effective assessment of need. Assessment of elderly persons needs in the community must include, at some stage, the contribution of the Doctor, Nurse and other para medics. At present many assessments are made and decisions acted upon without the involvement of the General Practitioner. Yet one of the most important causes of disorder in old age is the improper prescription and injection of drugs. The frequencies of side effects of drugs increases with old age. The physical condition and medication taken by the elderly are paramount issues in any assessment. Yet many staff ignore them or are unable to get the information from the Doctor.

To get an overall picture of the client and their needs the assessment must therefore be multidisciplinary. The same priority and resources must be brought to bear to assessment methods for the elderly as allocated to the present childrens service. The facilities of the Community Care Centre for the elderly, that I will outline in Chapter Eight would go some way to rectifying the situation.

The lack of training or education for the staff working in the domiciliary care field is to be deplored and is most surely one of the causes of the under-development of the service. A number of Agencies are at present responsible for the monitoring and development of training. The Central Council for Training and Education in Social Work (CCETSW) states that it has statutory responsibility for the training of Domiciliary Care Staff. However, the Local Government Training Board (LGTB) develops training programmes for care assistants in residential homes and also home helps. The training of both groups of staff is extremely variable. Some Local Authorities organise basic in service training others provide a more structured programme with the co-operation of local colleges. Many authorities have no training facilities or a very limited programme for home helps or care assistants. The managers of both domiciliary and residential care schemes have similar varied training opportunities. These programmes vary in quality and content.

The Certificate in Social Service, a non professional qualifying social work course validated by CCETSW is available to all non field social work staff. This includes both domiciliary and residential care staff. Many care assistants and some domiciliary organisers have completed the course but no home help has ever done so.

The Diploma of the Institute of Home Help Organisers and the Diploma or Certificate in Management Studies are also offered for Domiciliary Organisers in local colleges on a one day a week basis. All the courses available to Domiciliary Staff are on a day release and last from two to three years.

Diagram 7.1 Present training opportunities for Domiciliary and Residential Staff

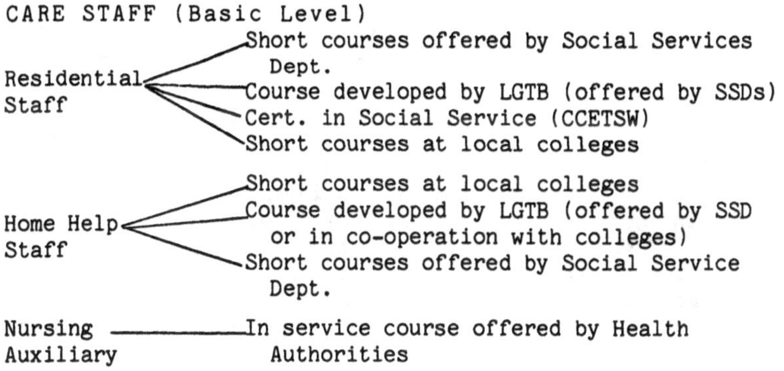

CARE STAFF (Basic Level)

Residential Staff
- Short courses offered by Social Services Dept.
- Course developed by LGTB (offered by SSDs)
- Cert. in Social Service (CCETSW)
- Short courses at local colleges

Home Help Staff
- Short courses at local colleges
- Course developed by LGTB (offered by SSD or in co-operation with colleges)
- Short courses offered by Social Service Dept.

Nursing Auxiliary
- In service course offered by Health Authorities

MANAGEMENT STAFF

Residential Care
- Cert. in Social Service (CCETSW)(Part-time)
- Cert. of Qualification in Social Work (CCETSW) (Full-time)
- In service Social Care Course (CCETSW) (One day a week at local college for one year)

Domiciliary Care
- Diploma of The Institute of Home Help Organisers (College course, or NALGO correspondence)
- Cert. in Social Service (CCETSW) (Part-time(
- Diploma or Certificate in Management Studies (Part-time)

Some Local Authorities encourage their staff to obtain one particular qualification. Others allow staff a choice. Diagram 7.1 does however show the diversity of training and training agencies involved in offering opportunities for domiciliary and residential care staff. Residential care staff can, however, progress through a stage by stage development programme, starting with short in-service courses, then progressing to the one year In Service Social Care Course at a local college and later, if appropriate, to a course offering the Certificate in Social Service or Certificate of Qualification in Social Work. This systemis not available to Domiciliary Home Helps or other basic level Domiciliary Staff, who have to content themselves with the luxury, of at most, a two week course at a local college with no opportunities for training or promotion after that. The part-time nature of the present home help role sometimes does not allow a member of staff the opportunity to leave home or attend college for long periods because of family commitment etc., but at the moment, with the influx of full-time posts, there is no reason why the same opportunities should not be offered.

The split in responsibility for training between CCETSW, LGTB and the Institute of Home Help Organisers militates against a comprehensive policy of training and development for Domiciliary Care Staff. CCETSW has never put the same effort into developing training programmes for Domiciliary Care Staff as they have expended on, for instance, Field Social Work or Residential and Day Care. They have not published one document on Domiciliary Care despite publishing many on Social Work, Day Care and Residential and Community Work. It is one example of their lack of interest in this field despite their statutory responsibility. The LGTB has produced training recommendation for care assistants and home helps, but it does not have the authority or resources to monitor them on a wide scale. As Domiciliary Care Work has not been defined as social work, although many of its tasks necessitate social work skills, it is difficult to see why CCETSW should wish to hold the statutory responsibility for training. The Barclay Report defined nearly every member of the Social Service Department as a social worker but did not mention the Domiciliary Organiser. The way, is therefore open, for a new form of training programme based on the needs of the future Domiciliary Organiser or Service Manager. In order for this to be facilitated the following is necessary:-

a. The removal of statutory responsibility from CCETSW for the training of Domiciliary Care Staff. As Loney points out CCETSW has become over the years more and more concerned with the "narrowing of the base of acceptable social work" pulling away from community work and more radical styles of social work.[68]

b. The formation of a new training agency with validating powers to develop and monitor training in this field. The members of this body would comprise of staff from colleges teaching the subject, members of the Institute of Home Help Organisers, Residential Care Association, Directors of Social Services and Students. If possible there should be representatives of the consumers of the service and local political representation through the various representative bodies.

c. A comprehensive training programme should be developed which will remove the class barriers between the home help and organiser. This would facilitate movement upwards by the home help into management posts if they have the ability and motivation.

d. (i) There must be offered a basic course for every member of staff irrespective of grade or post. The subjects covered would include Health Care, Health and Safety, Lifting etc., Needs of the Elderly in the Community, working as a team and knowledge of other agencies.

   (ii) A second tier programme should be available for those staff who have the potential to be Organisers. This would be a part-time course on much the same organisational lines as the present Certificate in Social Service. Two days at study and three days at work in the agency. The content would be work skill orientated and planned in close co-operation with agencies. Subjects covered would include:- Human Growth and Development, Social Administration and Social Policy, Legal Studies, Personnel Management and Health and Safety at Work, Interviewing Techniques, Assessment Methods and Implementation of Programmes and Self Awareness.

(iii) The qualification awarded would be equal in status to the CQSW.

(iv) There would be opportunity for post graduate training in management to enable Domiciliary Staff to compete for senior posts in Social Service Departments.

This system would help to overcome the cinderella attitude of the staff in the present service. They would have their basic training needs met and also have a professional training equal in status to other workers in the Department. Most important, of course, the client would benefit from such a programme as they would be offered help and support from trained and motivated staff.

<u>Summary</u>

I have in this chapter tried to draw together the rather diverse threads which run through the attempts of various bodies to organise training programmes for both the Domiciliary Organiser and the home help. In many areas of training, particularly of the home help, I have put forward that we have not progressed since the beginning of the century. Since the 1950s many attempts have been made to draw up appropriate training schemes for Organisers, but despite this, different Local Authorities still demand different qualifications for their staff. The Central Council for Training and Education in Social Work has not paid much attention to the training of Organisers despite taking statutory responsibility for their training. Brewer and Lait in their excellent book 'Can Social Work Survive' allege that CCETSW has proved to be an "expensive and arguably, superfluous body".[69] With this sentiment I wholeheartedly agree as far as their training initiatives for domiciliary care staff is concerned. Until perhaps an agreement can be reached as to the role and status of the domiciliary organiser, there will continue to be uncertainty about training objectives.

The introduction of the Certificate in Social Service as a qualification for all caring staff in social services other than field social workers, has been a controversial issue. Many staff still see the Certificate in Social Services as a second rate qualification. The present system of having two different qualifications for staff in social services only preserves the split and rivalry between workers in the different fields of social work. CCETSW argues that for holders of the Certificate in Social Service to do the work of posts which should be filled by holders of the Certificate of Qualification in Social Work would be to dilute standards,[70] only adds fuel to the argument as to the status of the qualifications. The evaluation of training policies carried out by CCETSW in 1983 showed all too clearly the divide in attitudes between the holders of the different qualifications. The British Association of Social Workers, the Universities and CQSW holders argue for the status quo.[71] In the present system training opportunities are offered to those who spend less and less time with clients such as field social workers, and very little training offered to those who spend most of their working day in direct contact with clients.

If we are concerned with the clients welfare this situation should cause some concern and soul searching as to the motives of those who argue for more and more training for the elite group, the social workers, in their drive for the status of 'professional'.

Notes

1. Training of Home Helps (Local Government Training Board, 1978).

2. Home Help Services in Great Britain (National Council of Home Help Service, 1979), Section 2.7.

3. See articles on manual workers in the Social Services, Community Care (15 July pp.16-17, 22 July pp.20-21, 29 July pp.22-24, 5 August pp.17-18 and 12 August pp.20-21, 1982).

4. L. Clarke, PhD. research material, Department of Sociological Studies, Sheffield University.

5. E. Younghusband, Social Workers in Britain (T & A Constable Ltd., London, 1951), para. 49, p.24.

6. Government Committee on the Prevention and Relief of Distress. Circular letter to Local

Representative Committees, No. 3, Local Government Board, 2 November 1914.

7. Report of the Womens Advisory Committee on the Domestic Service Problems, Ministry of Reconstruction, Cmd. 67, 1919, p.4.

8. N. Malin, 'Group Homes for Mentally Handicapped Adults', unpublished PhD. Thesis, 1980, University of Sheffield.

9. Womens Advisory Committee, 1919, p.8.

10. Ibid., p.13.

11. Report of the Committee on Domestic Service, Ministry of Labour, HMSO, 1923.

12. Ibid., p.10.

13. Ibid., p.13.

14. See G. Sumner, R. Smith, _Planning Local Authority Services for the Elderly_ (George Allen and Unwin, London, 1969), p.235.

15. Report on the Post-War Organisation of Private Domestic Employment, Ministry of Labour and National Service, Cmd. 6650, HMSO, 1945.

16. D.M. Elliott, 'The Status of Domestic Work in the United Kingdom', _International Labour Review_, Geneva, Vol. LXIII, No. 2 (Feb. 1951), p.144.

17. Ibid., p.144.

18. N. Burr, _The Home Help Service_ (Henry G. Morris, London, 1949), p.33-34.

19. Ibid., p.34-38.

20. Ibid., p.34.

21. The Institute of Home Help Organisers organise a two year part-time training course. The Central Council for Training and Education in Social Work also provides for the training of domiciliary care staff in the Certificate in Social Service schemes. See the Evidence of the Institute of Home Help Organisers to the Working Party on the Role of the Social Worker (Barclay Report), _The Newsletter_ (8 August 1981).

22. A.I. Harris, _Meals on Wheels for Old People_ (National Corporation for the Care of Old People, London, 1960).

23. Source: WVS course for Home Help Organisers 26 April to 30 April, 1948, Leatherhead, in draft minutes and reports, City of Sheffield, No. 103, Health Committee 22 April to 10 June 1948, File No. CA 164/159.

24. Ibid., p.6.

25. Report of the Working Party on Social Workers in Local Authority Health and Welfare Services Ministry of Health 1959.

26. Ibid., para. 480.

27. Ibid., para. 678.

28. Sumner and Smith, *Local Authority Services*, p.234.

29. Ibid., p.235.

30. Ibid., p.235.

31. J. Parker, 'The Trained Home Help in the Domiciliary Services', *The Medical Officer*, Vol. CXIX, No. 7 (1968).

32. Ibid., p.85.

33. P. Evans, 'Training in the Home Help Service', *British Journal and Social Service Review* (24 June 1972).

34. Review of the Home Help Service in England July 1972. Social Work Service, DHSS, 1973.

35. Ibid., p.92.

36. Institute of Home Help Organisers, Annual Report, 1981-82, p.9.

37. M.E. Turner, 'Helping the Home Help', *Nursing Times*, Vol. 67, No. 10 (1971), pp.287-289.

38. Review of the Home Help Service, 1973, p.84.

39. Report of the working party on the Home Help Service in Milton Keynes (Buckinghamshire County Council, 1973).

40. Report of Joint Working Party, Training for Organisers of Home Help and Other Supportive Services. CCETSW and Local Government Training Board (1974), p.17.

41. M. Fitzgerald, 'Training Home Help Organisers', *Local Government Chronicle* (11 July 1975), p.669.

42. Report of Joint Working Party, 1974, see para. 4 and para. 8.

43. Ibid., Addendum to the report. See also statement by CCETSW, November 1976.

44. Statutory Instrument 1265/74, CCETSW order, 1974.

45. Fitzgerald, 'Training Home Help Organisers', p.668.

46. Ibid., p.668.

47. Gwynedd County Council, *A Research Review of the Operation of the Home Help Service in Gwynedd* (The Council, Caernavon, 1977).

48. Institute of Home Help Organisers, *The Journal*, Vol. 22, Issue 67 (Dec. 1974), p.23.

49. Ibid., p.20.

50. Ibid., p.25.

51. CSS progress report, CCETSW paper 9:4, 1980.

52. Ibid., p.46.

53. DHSS Manpower and Training for the Social Services (HMSO, London, 1976).

54. Training of Home Helps, Training Recommendation No. 22, Local Government Training Board (1978).

55. Ibid., p.4.

56. 'Training for Social Services', Local Government Training Board Newsletter, Special Issue (May 1982).

57. Ibid., L. Bell and R. Douglase, p.5.

58. See C. Brewer and J. Lait, Can Social Work Survive? (Temple Smith, London, 1980).

59. Training for Social Service, 1982, p.6.

60. Council of Europe, Committee of Ministers, Resolution (77) 37, para. 4.

61. M. Nordstrom, 'Reasons for Assistance - Task of the Home Help', in Proceedings of the International Congress on the Home Help Services 1965 (U.S. Department of Health Education and Welfare, Washington D.C., W.A. publication No. 17, 1966).

62.See La Profession, Travailleuse Familiale, Conference de Presse du 13 Juin 1967 and Travailleuse Familiales, Issues No. 25-26 (Decembre 1966, Mars 1967), F.N.A.P.A.F. 1 Rue de Maubeuge, Paris IX.

63. M. Nordstrom, 'Social Home Help Service in Sweden', International Labour Review, Vol. LXXXVIII (July-Dec. 1963), pp.357-369.

64. A. Smith, 'A Fellow Traveller in Sweden', The Newsletter, The Institute of Home Help Organisers (September 1980), p.2.

65. A. Maddock, 'Dutch Treat', The Newsletter, The Institute of Home Help Organisers (July 1977), p.2.

66. F. Clarke, 'Hospital at Home - Patient Choice - the French Connection', Concord, No. 8 (Spring 1977), pp.21.25.

67. Implementation of a Home Help Service (Dublin Council for the Aged, Dublin, 1972).

68. M. Loney, Community Care (21 July 1983).

69. C. Brewer and J. Lait, Can Social Work Survive? (Temple Smith, London, 1980).

70. CCETSW, The Certificate in Social Service, paper 9:1 (CCETSW, London, 1975), p.7.

71. CCETSW Review of Qualifying Training Policies, paper 20 (CCETSW, London, 1983).

Chapter Eight

THE FUTURE OF DOMICILIARY CARE

What of the future? Has Domiciliary Care a part to play in the care of the elderly in their own homes? At present Domiciliary Services are a major support to a small number of very dependent elderly people. The number of persons helped by the service is small compared to the number supported by relatives, friends and volunteers. However, in terms of Social Service Departments the Domiciliary Services form a large proportion of the total number of clients referred. The Service forms by far the largest Social Services support to the elderly in the community.

I am particularly aware of the complexity of argument about service delivery in social service departments. As an ex senior manager I am all too aware of the complex nature of bureaucrat organisations. For this reason I try in this chapter to give a clear argument as to how services for the elderly should develop. The reader should bear in mind that what I propose should be seen against the organisation of service for children and other groups.

A number of experimental Community Social Service projects at present in the embryo stages may have a very profound effect upon the organisation and kind of Domiciliary Services which will be provided in the next 20 years. The move in some Social Service Departments to the service delivery system known as 'patchwork', which is basically the provision of services with the maximum involvement of the local community at a local level, if developed effectively, has the potential to make Domiciliary Services the kingpin in the support offered to the elderly. The major drawback as far as Domiciliary Services are concerned is that in all the 'patch' experiments it has been automatically assumed without question that a qualified field social worker would lead the team. I shall later in this chapter examine in more detail this system and its possible effect upon the development of Domiciliary Services. One of the other policy developments which may also affect the development of domiciliary care services is the move away from residential care, with the transfer of resources to new methods of bringing services to the elderly in their own homes. Before I discuss the future for Domiciliary Services and the possible effects of the new policies of Social Services, Housing and Health Services, I would like to look briefly at the present system of support for elderly persons and the events that have shaped that system. In the past 80 years have we moved very much? Are many of the elderly today still living in the same conditions as before the introduction of the Welfare State? Do the present community services reach those in most need in their own homes? There is much evidence to support the view that they do not. This evidence, it would seem, only surfaces when a crisis arises or an old person is found in need. A point most vividly illustrated by the following example: "The old woman's deterioration was such that her condition was desperate. She was found slumped in a broken, urine-saturated armchair in front of an empty firegrate. The day was bitterly cold and she had no fuel... Nor had she any food... her person was filthy, face and hands showing embedded dirt. Her hair was lousey and her clothing foul rags... her three roomed flat... its walls covered in soot and dirt, streaked with excreta and hung with cobwebs... The old woman slept in a chair in front of the fire... The food cupboard by the side of the fireplace was quite bare".[1] This 80 year old lady had no sheets or blankets, her toilet facilities were on the landing of her accommodation. She had no electric heating as the wiring was too dangerous. This, unfortunately is not an extract from evidence to the 1909 Poor Law Commission, but a description of an elderly person's situation in the 1970s, a situation, which, no doubt, still exists in many Authorities today. As a result of this lady's position the local newspaper surveyed the City of Sheffield and found 1,300 other elderly persons in similar conditions. These old persons lived in one of the most progressive Cities in the United Kingdom, which has always spent more than the national average on services for the elderly. What of the elderly who live in the majority of Cities who spend less on services for the elderly? It is obvious that even when a Local Authority spends money on services many old people slip through the net or refuse care. It is quite clear that Social Service Departments are failing to support many of the elderly. Their last years are not as happy as possible, not without pain and many suffer isolation and loss of freedom.

Many argue that residential care is the appropriate form of care for those elderly persons who cannot at present look after themselves without help and support in their own homes. Studies have, however, shown that residential care is not only inappropriate but positively harmful and should be the last resort available only to a small minority of elderly persons who have either decided to enter care, or who cannot look after themselves with the support of friends, relatives or Domiciliary Services. Residential care as organised and managed today, is, and should be seen as, second best to imaginative support in the community. The dangers for the old person who has to endure the admission process and residential care are highlighted by Goffman, Robb and others.[2]

"Institutions develop powerful instruments of defence for their protection and perpetuation. Sometimes their officers or governing bodies lose sight of the primary purpose for which they were planned and their energies become deployed in rituals or personality conflicts. The purpose becomes subordinated to the personnel."[3]

Many residential homes for the elderly still display the various rituals whose sole purpose is to strip the old person of all individuality so that they conform to the regime of the institution. The studies by Townsend and Robb reinforced this view.[4] Townsend argues that the treatment in some residential establishments runs counter to good practices. He recommends that the elderly be allowed to stay in their own homes. "Communal Homes" he states "of this kind which exist in England and Wales today do not adequately meet the physical, psychological and social need of the elderly people living in them, and......alternative services and living arrangements should quickly take their place." Since Townsend's study many other researchers have attempted to measure the effects of such institutions upon elderly residents. Some like Bennett and Nahemow have argued that the bad effects of the institutions upon residents might have been caused by the "lack of clarity of expection, or even absence of any expection of adjustment".[5] Jenkins in a later study found that many elderly peoples experience of residential homes "reduces the need to engage in many practical activities of daily living, all too often it also fails to provide the chance to engage in them at all, or in alternative recreational activities".[6] Many old people experience great pain and stress during and after the admission process. One of the most common and damaging characteristics of the admission process is the invasion of the elderly person's privacys. Many old people do not adjust to this invasion upon their dignity and display symptoms of withdrawal, uninterest, apathy and submissiveness. Yawney and Slover in 1973 vividly showed this process. Residential care has been described as the interval between social and physical death.[7]

Many staff, at all levels of management in Social Service Departments are either unaware of these dangers or do little to overcome them. Many social workers do not prepare their clients for the trauma of admission and once the client is admitted they are removed from the social worker's caseload. This, of course, only reinforces the view to the client that she or he has been put away and forgotten. The gap in understanding between workers in residential care and field social work is, perhaps, wider than that between field workers and domiciliary workers. In a national survey of care assistants in residential homes for the elderly preliminary results indicate that it is very rare for residential staff to be involved in observing residents, writing reports, or attending supervision sessions or reviews of residents. All this supports the view that in many homes the resident is not viewed as a person who can be helped to function at a higher level than at admission. The whole emphasis is on physical care. Very few homes have plans to develop the residents' abilities or to help them lead a full and independent a life as possible within their capabilities.[8] Even if residential care can be justified for a small number of elderly persons, it must be made a supportive experience. To do this would involve a massive input into the training and development of all grades of staff in the service and a change of attitude on the part of social workers in the field. Social workers have a part to play in the assessment of those clients on their own caseloads who may wish or need residential care, but for the majority who are not on their caseloads, the residential and domiciliary staff should play a larger part than at present in the assessment and admission process. Unless the old person is ill and cannot be nursed at home, there is no reason to prevent them being looked after at home if appropriate domiciliary facilities are used imaginatively. A few authorities are trying to help their staff alleviate the stresses and problems of institutionalisation both for the staff and residents, but despite this awareness of the damaging effect of residential care, recent research by Godlove, Richard and Rodwell,[9] shows all too vividly the uselessness of attempting changes. This study highlights the dangers of residential care, the lack of privacy, loss of individuality, and the lack of interest by many staff in the residents' welfare. A few of their observations will help to illustrate my point. "Lunch time in a residential home. A care assistant brings lunch to a resident who is sitting with her hands clasped on the table. Without looking at what she is doing she puts the plate on the resident's folded hands and leaves. Not a word is spoken". This observation says much about the lack of communication between residents and staff, lack of care and understanding on the part of the staff and the absence of any effective supervision on the part of management. The fact that it occurred when staff knew they were being observed by researchers requires no comment. Many other more serious occurrences were reported, typical of which was an incident where the care assistant wheeled an elderly lady into the lounge of a home and answered the resident's request to go to the toilet by saying "you're in the lounge now" and calling her by the wrong name. The old lady was left to sit in pain and humiliation for the afternoon. Every social worker, be they voluntary or statutory, field or domiciliary or residential should read the following account from the same study of the admission to residential care of an elderly person.

"It is half past eleven in an old peoples' home. The morning drinks have been taken, and the cups collected. In a small lounge with fire doors at each end, ten old ladies are sitting quietly along two walls. Some are staring ahead of them and some appear to be dozing. Through one of the fire doors comes a member of staff carrying a small suitcase. Behind her is a thin old man holding a hat in front of him with both hands. In the room she turns, asks him to sit in a vacant chair, places the suitcase in front of him, and goes out through the other door. The old man is dressed in a dark suit with a white shirt, dark tie, and polished black shoes. The suit is cut in a very old style and has been carefully pressed which makes him look as though he is on his way to a Sunday Service or a funeral. He holds the hat very tightly in his lap and his hands are shaking. Some of the old ladies glance at him and then look away. After several minutes of silence another staff member comes in carrying a piece of paper and a pen, reads an address to him, and asks if that is the correct address of his next of kin. He clears his throat and says it is. After she has gone, he sits forward stiffly in the chair, gazing at the floor in front of his suitcase. Ten minutes elapse. The first member of staff returns with a cup of tea and asks if he would like sugar. He shakes his head. She hands him the cup of tea and departs again. As he sits holding his hat and the cup, the shaking of his hand make the cup rattle loudly. It is the only sound. He sips quickly at the tea. Before he can finish, the staff member returns, says that his room is ready, picks up his suitcase and goes through the door holding it open for him. He rises quickly to his feet, holding his hat and half finished cup of tea and looks around. There are no tables in the room and he balances the cup on a window ledge behind the seat before hurrying out of the room. The old ladies who have looked up at his departure return their gaze to the walls and floors."

I may be accused of being selective in my examples of the effects upon both staff and residents of the residential care system. I make no apology for being selective. I wish to make a point. The disturbing effects of residential care have been documented for over a hundred years, yet we still continue to place people in these situations. Effective domiciliary care is, at the present time, the only form of support that will allow both the staff and clients to retain their dignity. I do not attach any blame to the staff, it is the Institutions. The very nature of Institutions means that one group has control or power over another and it will nearly always be misused and abused. History has taught us this. I believe that it is well neigh impossible to prevent the institutionalisation of staff and residents and that the only alternative is not to place people in those situations and look after them in their own homes.

As the swing away from residential care gains momentum and the number of elderly persons over 75 years increases, the need for Domiciliary Services becomes all too obvious.

It is well established that there is a shortfall

in the provision of services to the elderly. The lack of clear statements on policy makes it difficult to do more than make general statements about these deficiences. In 1979, Chapman[10] reported a shortfall in health and welfare services to over half the elderly persons covered by his survey. Many elderly people, at the present time, see residential care as the only way to meet their needs, but there is a high degree of unmet need among those elderly frail dependent people who choose to stay in their own homes.[11] The latest survey of the elderly in the community supports this view.[12] One third of those over 65 live alone and just over one third live with an elderly spouse. The proportion of those living alone increases commensurate with advancing years. At least seven out of ten elderly persons live in households where there is no one under 65, and many of those living alone do not have relatives living nearby, are less likely to have the use of telephones, washing machines or vacuum cleaners. They live in old accommodation. About one tenth of those interviewed were unable to leave their homes and, of those over 85 years of age, almost one half were unable to do so. One disturbing fact to emerge was that many people over 75 are unable to get around their own homes or get in or out of bed without help. Many of the elderly were also unable to carry out domestic or personal tasks such as washing themselves, cutting toenails, preparing food, or actually feeding themselves. For those living alone the most frequent source of help is Domiciliary Services such as home help and Meals on Wheels. Only one in ten who live alone received this service. Once again this survey only serves to highlight the sorry plight of the elderly and the paramount importance of developing adequate Domiciliary Services to meet their needs.

I hope that I have shown in chapters one to three how the services for the elderly grew, not in response to Central Government planning and foresight but in response to immediate crises. Many of the major developments grew as a result of the development of other services. Meals on Wheels, home helps for the elderly and many other important services were a result of wartime conditions not long term planning. One of the major defects of this lack of Central Government initiative is the piecemeal development of services, unco-ordinated, and varying in both quality and quantity. An example of the lack of the Department of Health and Social Security's concern is that no one person on their

Social Work Advisory Staff has full time responsibility for the monitoring or development of Domiciliary Services at a National level. This is despite the fact that Domiciliary Services play such a large part in Social Service provision and, perhaps, in most authorities is the biggest spender. The reorganisation of the personal Social Services in 1972 did not alleviate many of the problems caused by duplication and unco-ordination of services for the elderly. Most of the services which they use today are still managed by different Central and Local Government Departments. Social Service Departments are responsible for Meals on Wheels, Home Helps, Day Centres, Social Work, Residential Care. The Housing Department responsible for sheltered housing and wardens. Health Authorities are responsible for Community Health and Nursing Services. Education Departments organise adult education and recreation facilities and County Councils local transport. Each of these departments may have a policy with respect to services for the elderly and most probably if it has, it has been drawn up in many cases without consultation with one or all of the other responsible bodies.

In many people's view, including the present writer's, the elderly living alone in the community is the single most pressing problem for today's society. How do we organise services to assist them to live a full life without removing their freedom of choice or dignity? Domiciliary Services play a small part but to be effective must be seen in conjunction with housing policies, recreation and education policies, if it is to be utilised by the elderly to the full. Supporting and providing services for the elderly is now the major role of many Social Service Departments. Domiciliary Services play a large part in that role and, in my view, is one of the most important functions of many Social Service Departments today. It is all the more deplorable that as a nation we keep no Health or Social Services statistics for the over 75 year olds and the amount of information requested on services for the elderly is being reduced by Central Government. This lack of information hampers management in their efforts to plan services.

From these perspectives a major element of the need to be more imaginative in the use of resources and the removal of outdated traditional models of care based on present departmental boundaries arises. A more flexible response to client need is necessary.

Over the past ten years one of the issues which

has been touched upon but on which very little serious discussion has been held, is who should be the person in the Social Service Department most suited to receive referrals and manage and co-ordinate services for the elderly? Who should be the 'gate keeper' as far as the over 65s are concerned. To date the social work profession sees the generic social worker as the 'gate keeper' for all referrals to the Social Services Department. Examination of Government Reports and Ministry Circulars provides no recommendations to support this position.[13] A recent book published titled 'Managing Social Work' (perhaps it should be more appropriately titled 'Managing Social Services') assumes without question that social workers are the natural inheritors of the right to lead Social Service Teams in Social Service Departments.[14] The majority of the workload in these teams is with the elderly. With the social work professions collective inexperience of working with the elderly, Domiciliary Care Staff should be considered to lead these teams. This trend to decentralisation, as it is being organised at present, is a danger to the efficient development of Domiciliary Services and could lead to the loss of the experience of the Domiciliary Organiser. Some of these trends in decentralisation in the social services are called 'patch work'. It is a concept which believes that services should be provided at a local level, with the involvement of the local community, using volunteers and recognising the value of the support provided by families and friends to clients. The statutory services support these informal carers not supplant them. To develop this concept to its limit requires a change in the organisation of present Social Service Departments, so as to delegate as much responsibility as possible to the 'patch' team consisting of social workers, domiciliary care staff and welfare assistants led by a social worker. This structure can react quickly to clients' requests and can utilise not only the departments' resources, but that of the local community also. At the present time however there is little involvement of the consumer in the management of the teams.

There are many different forms of decentralisation of which 'patch' is but one. Decentralisation may mean decentralisation of service delivery (patch), decentralisation of decision making or resource allocation as in the Kent Community Care project, described later, or neighbourhood centres as developed in some London Boroughs.

All the reported experiments providing this form of care are being managed by social workers.[15] Many of the teams have excluded work with children and spend most of their efforts working with the elderly, handicapped, mentally ill and mentally handicapped. The present responsibilities of the team leader points to the necessity for some one to fill the post who is expert in assessment procedures, management of staff and allocating resources. Most of these roles the qualified social worker has not experienced, but all of them have been the responsibility of the Domiciliary Care Organiser. Goldberg in 1979[16] after reviewing the work of social workers with the elderly, concluded that "it would be unrealistic to imagine that it is possible or even desirable for trained social workers to carry out such assessments". She was referring to assessment for Domiciliary Services. This statement I would support. However by 1982 Goldberg[17] had changed her opinion and had reached the conclusion that social workers were able to carry out nearly every role in Social Service Departments. She saw the social worker as the 'gate keeper' in the department, mobilising resources, assessing all referrals, carrying out treatment programmes, i.e. case work. The social worker would also co-ordinate and monitor service delivery systems (some of which could be delegated to Home Help Organisers) and also act as consultants or resource persons to others in the department. They would also function as community workers. None of these functions are the prerogative of the qualified or unqualified social worker. These functions can and are being carried out effectively by other workers. Hey in 1980 argued that the attitudes of social workers to their 'gate keeper' role was wrong. She found that social workers are not trained or able to assess basic service (Domiciliary Services) needs. Nor have they the relevant experience to bring to the role.[18]

A minority of social workers have however attempted to introduce new methods of working with the elderly. One particular innovation is that of the Kent Community Care Project. The philosophy of the scheme has been taken up and implemented by one or two other Local Authorities. The main object of the Kent scheme and its imitators, is an attempt by authorities to be more cost effective, flexible and also to strengthen the family and community ties. "The mechanics adopted to achieve these aims was the provision of a decentralised budget to experienced social workers who would take the responsibility for the co-ordination and development of care for the elderly people". The project hoped to keep elderly people, who would normally require residential care, in the community. Social workers involved in the scheme assess the clients needs and the resources available in the community which might meet some of those needs. Social workers with their allocated budget, buy resources in the community to support the elderly person. Challis and Davis[19] who have monitored the project found that it was beneficial to clients in particular those who were highly dependent. There was also a lower rate of admission to residential homes than in the control group. Without doubt this project is a move in the right direction. This scheme and others like it seems to have had limited success. Would they have been more successful if they had been managed by experienced Domiciliary Workers?

To provide an alternative to the present inadequate care system for the elderly it is necessary to re-think how best to provide support without the unnecessary restrictions of present departmental boundaries. It is necessary to break down departmental boundaries in order to provide a co-ordinated, comprehensive and effective community care support system to elderly persons. Any new development must have as its starting point, the concept that elderly people have a basic right to live in their own homes with all that that implies. Their right to take risks, to have control over their own lives, to enjoy privacy and choice, and be allowed to participate in the development of policy and management of the service. Local Governments must now begin to examine the limitations of its departmental structures if they are to make a comprehensive community care system for the elderly a possibility. The present departmental structure of Central and Local Government militates against any real initiative because of the restricted bureaucratic nature of the organisation. The present structure of Local Government owes more to the needs of the 19th century and the outdated need for professional groups to have control over their own development. There is no longer a need, as far as the consumer is concerned, for the various professionals to provide services in isolation from other departments and statutory agencies. The present organisation of Local Government allows no one department to have the necessary resources to support any one group of client or consumer. Each department provides only part of the overall service to various groups. The elderly are provided for by the Education Department, Social Service Department, Housing Department, Libraries and Health Authorities. Transport policies of course do not often take account of the needs of the elderly.

Each department has structures which in many cases do not allow different sections to co-operate as they would wish and many groups do not, co-operate because of professional and territorial jealousies. No one section of the Social Service Department has the resources, either in terms of personnel or expertise, to allow the elderly a true choice of care. Many, if not all, elderly persons who are in residential care suffer the indignities of that system because of the inability of present community services to cope with their individual needs. All old people require that their basic needs are met. All require appropriate accommodation and some require personal, medical, nursing and domestic help. Every person requires food, warmth and contact with others in the community. At present many organisations try to meet these needs in isolation, but as elderly persons needs may change suddenly, consequently they need appropriate services quickly. Under the present system because of the number of agencies and personnel involved, these needs, if met at all, are not met quickly enough. Many old people fall through the welfare net as no one organisation or agency has sole responsibility for seeing that services are offered.

Earlier in this chapter the inadequacies and problems associated with residential care were pointed out. Consequently any new system must take the services to the elderly persons in their own homes. Not the client to the service. Research in progress points to the fact that the role of Domiciliary Care Staff, Residential Care Staff and Auxiliary Nursing Staff in the Community, are all providing substantially the same form of support to the elderly with differences only in intensity and setting. All of these personnel carry out domestic tasks, personal caring such as bathing, feeding, dressing-undressing clients, applying simple dressing and administering simple medication. All help the client with emotional support and advice and help with shopping, budgeting etc. These preliminary results, from over 100 Health Authorities and 25 Social Service Departments point to the overlap of roles and waste of resources through lack of co-ordination and co-operation between services. The results also point to the fact that the support given to clients in residential care could, in most cases, be given more effectively in the clients' own home.[20] What is required, therefore, is a completely different concept of service delivery to elderly persons in their own homes. One that combines the functions of the different groups at present providing care, which is organised to meet the needs of recipients rather than the needs of departmentalism, professional idiosyncracies or trade unions.

This could be achieved if staff in Local Government agreed to forget their need for departmentalism and agreed to provide all services to the elderly in the community through local centres. These centres would co-ordinate and provide all the necessary resources to enable the elderly person to live a safe and enriched life in their own homes. An appropriate title for such units would be Neighbourhood Support Units. The unit could be situated in either existing or new purpose built accommodation. The unit or centre would be equipped to provide both meals on wheels and cafeteria facilities for those elderly persons who wished to make use of them. The premises would also be equipped to provide domiciliary services, district nursing, chiropody, social work, bathing facilities and physiotherapy. It would also act as a local advice centre for the elderly, providing advice on a wide range of issues. Facilities would also be available to enable the elderly to take part and enjoy recreational activities, cultural activities and hobbies. The facilities of the Centre would be open to all the elderly in the neighbourhood without any assessment procedure as to eligibility. Only the 24 hour Community Support Service would be subject to assessment. One of the most important and essential services to be provided within this scheme would be this 24 hour Domiciliary Care Support to the elderly who wished to stay in their own homes. Community Care Assistant Staff carrying out the duties of the existing three groups of staff, Home Helps, Residential Care Assistants and Community Nursing Auxiliaries, would provide a domestic, personal and emotional support service to the elderly. For the elderly who are frail, handicapped or ill an alarm system, connected to the Centre would be provided.

The overall aim of the new system, and in particular the Community Care Scheme, would be one of flexibility. Flexibility both in staff attitudes, ability and service delivery. For those few elderly who would wish to or have to enter residential care the centre would provide assessment facilities and small residential units could be attached to the centre managed by the Centre Organiser.

This volume is concerned with services for the elderly only and I therefore have not gone in any detail as to how the Centre would relate to other groups of clients such as children, mentally ill or handicapped. I believe that each group of clients need their own specialist response from Social Service Departments in contrast to the present generic approach. The Centre would provide the following services which are at present offered by a number of different agencies and within those agencies in different sections.

Present Service	Agency providing service at present	Service to be provided by Neighbourhood Support Unit
Home Help	SSD Domiciliary Care) Sect.)	
Res.Care	SSD Residential Sect)	Community Care
Nursing Aux.	Health Auth. Nursing) Division)	Assistant
Meals on Wheels	SSD Domiciliary Care Sect.	Meals on Wheels
Luncheon Club	SSD - Voluntary	Cafeteria 8am - 8pm.
Chiropody	Health Authority	Domiciliary Chiropody and at Centre
Laundry	Some SSD Domiciliary Sect.	Domiciliary and facility at Centre
Hairdressing	SSD Day Care Sect.	Domiciliary and facility at Centre
Physiotherapy	Health Authority	Domiciliary and facility at Centre
District Nurse	Health Authority Nusing Div.	Domiciliary and facility at Centre
Library	Library Dept.)	Hobbies, education and
Recreation	Recreation Dept.)	recreation facilities
Education	Education Dept.)	offered by statutory and voluntary agencies
Housing Rights	)	
Advice	Housing Dept.)	
Welfare Benefits	)	
Advice	Social Service Dept.)	Unified Rights
Legal Advice	Citizens Advice) Bureau)	Advice Service
Consumer Advice	Consumer protection) service of County) Councils)	

Present Service	Agency providing service at present	Service to be provided by Neighbourhood Support Unit
Tranport	Social Service Dept.	Domiciliary Transport System
Residential Care	Social Service Dept. Residential Care Section	Small Residential Care Unit.

The Community Care Assistant support service would provide the following services to complement the facilities at the Centre.

a. Support: Befriend and adviser to the elderly. The Community Care Assistant would in many cases be the only contact with the community and other agencies that the elderly person may need.

b. Instructor and Teacher
The Community Care Assistant may have to support many elderly persons after the death of a spouse or close friend who has lived with them. Men in particular have very little idea of shopping, cooking and cleaning and would need help in making decisions and instruction in cooking, cleaning and budgeting etc. The staff would also in some cases provide a reliable and dependable figure for the client to relate to until they can feel confident enough to cope without support again.

c. Motivator: Rehabilitator: Therapist
At present many Home Helps fulfil these functions although they are not officially in their job descriptions. The Community Care Assistants could help to overcome the old person's feeling of isolation and stimulate them into overcoming many of the problems associated with the onset of old age. The stimulus of a visit can often motivate the old person into activity and this can be built upon to encourage them to do things for themselves. With support the Community Care Assistant can take on a therapeutic role either to support a social worker or physiotherapist or on their own behalf with instruction.

d. Nurse and Domestic Help
The Community Care Assistant would provide many of the services now provided by both the Home Help and Nursing Auxiliary. They would administer medicines, bath clients and also give bed-baths, empty catheter bags, apply

simple dressings, clean incontinent clients, prepare special meals and feed clients. This amalgamating of the roles of both workers overcomes many of the problems of overlap at present in the system.

e. Advocate
At present the Home Help is the only person who is in a position to request services from other agencies for many clients and on occasion to represent clients at tribunals. For the housebound the Home Help is also the only source of information about services or benefits available. This service would be encouraged by the new scheme on a large scale.

f. Monitor
Most Social Service and Local Authority personnel such as social workers, meals on wheels drivers and rent collectors carry out this function to some extent. However, the Community Care Assistant as far as the elderly are concerned can provide a vital service by monitoring their condition for or on behalf of doctors, nurses and generally reporting to their superiors any deterioration or change in the client's condition. The visitor may also deal with any emergencies that arise by calling to the client the appropriate help, be it plumber or doctor.

The services to be provided would be determined by the clients' condition and wishes. Many who would otherwise be in residential care may need 24 hour cover. They may need help to get out of bed and dress in the morning, have their fires lit, food prepared for both breakfast, dinner and tea. They may also need putting to bed in the evening. Other clients may only need a domestic cleaning or laundry service. The value of the proposed system is its flexibility and range of services that can be provided to meet individual needs. It allows the client to have their freedom and to choose and discuss their needs with staff.

The manager or organiser of the 24 hour Community Care Scheme is one of the vital cogs in the system. He or she would need to be adaptable, with imagination and initiative and not hampered by tradition. Many existing Domiciliary Care Staff could fulfil this role but others are, unfortunately, too bound up in the traditional home help role. Skills in management, assessment, analysis, development of treatment programmes and ability to co-ordinate, discuss and articulate client need to other agencies would be the qualities needed for the post.

Management skills are important as the Organiser would have many Community Care Assistants to co-ordinate, motivate and communicate with. The Organiser would also be responsible for the allocation of work to Assistants and the communication of each client's need to the staff and for the monitoring of the quality of service given. Assessment skills would be a pre-requisite of the post, as the holder would be responsible for the assessment of client need in consultation with the client and the appropriate agencies. This involves the gathering of information, interpreting different pieces of information, discussing and weighing up the significance of the information and courses of action and the monitoring of the agreed action. The skill of collaborating with colleagues and agencies is also essential.

The Organiser would be responsible and accountable for all the clients on their caseload. They would therefore be called to account for the exercise of the professional judgement. They would be responsible for assessing clients' needs and also for seeing that those needs are met. They would therefore be accountable for seeing that the client received other appropriate services such as Meals on Wheels, Chiropody, Social Work etc. To provide for the essential client and community participation, the Organiser would be responsible for a small geographical area of the locality. This would facilitate the acquisition of relevant knowledge of the neighbourhood and also enable the Organiser to know of and have recourse to local resources. The Organiser would need an intimate knowledge of the benefits and rights available to the elderly and of other agencies serving the elderly so as to be able to call in as necessary such help. The Organiser could, for instance, call in the services of a social worker or other specialist.

The Barcley Report on the role and tasks of social workers saw them as having the responsibility for social casework and also planning of services. The report was not in agreement on the role and tasks of social workers and was split as to whether social work was confined to casework or wider community involvement.[21] I would support one of the minority reports which puts forward the view that social workers should restrict their role to that of caseworkers. It is this service that I would expect the Community Care Organiser to refer elderly clients for if appropriate.

An elderly person would have direct access to all the facilities provided at the Centre.

The Community Care Organiser would assess and review all elderly clients for the Community Care Support Service in clients' own homes and those clients who wished to be considered for residential care.

The Centre Manager would co-ordinate the work of the different professional groups working from the Centre. The skill to motivate staff from such wide and diverse backgrounds and co-ordinate these services in the best interests of the client would be the most important skill necessary for the post. In my view no particular professional qualification would be necessary but training in management would be essential, as would a sensitive understanding of professional issues.

The scheme would not only provide a more efficient and effective service to clients than at present, but it would also provide a career structure for staff, as any one of the staff involved in the service, provided they had the personal qualities and management qualifications, would be eligible for consideration for the post of Manager of the Centre. The scheme also allows for the maximum community participation and involvement of Voluntary Agencies. It provides for the maximum public participation without the assumption that the leader of any new social service innovation must be a qualified social worker. It allows for none of the obsessions of staff in Social Service Departments over the past few years with qualifications, specialisations and preservation of professional boundaries. The Centre staff would also be in a position to offer support to the providers of informal care such as neighbours, family and friends of the elderly.

The policy making structure of the centre I have left until last to put forward because it is important that all those who provide services and those who received them should play a part in the decision making process. The elderly are in a weak bargaining position for many reasons. They must be given their right to control their own future. The Centre could play a role in fostering the elderly persons self-assertiveness. This can in my view only be done by examining local decision making systems and giving the elderly a bigger part to play in them.

Diagram 8.1 Referral System: Neighbourhood Support Units Elderly

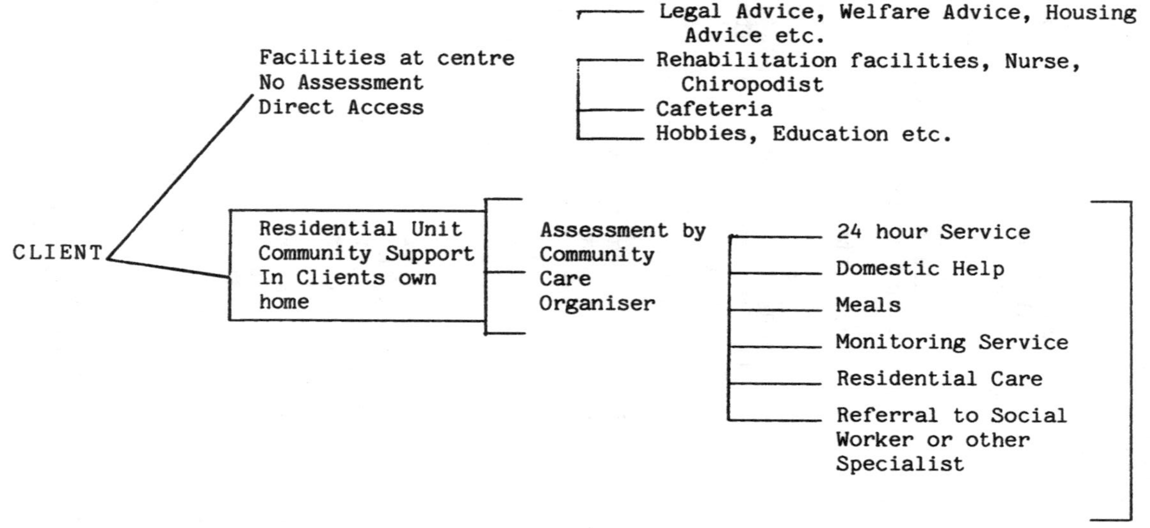

The elderly must have a larger voice in management and decision making of the services which they use. The staff of the Centre would, of course, be responsible to a Chief Officer for discipline and execution of the policy and the appropriate Service Committee. However, to encourage the maximum participation of all involved, the day to day policy decisions would be made by a committee comprised of staff, volunteers, local councillors and consumers. This arrangement would provide checks and balances so that no group or profession could impose their values or attitudes on the clients or rest of the staff. The committee would not only be responsible for the day to day running of the Centre but also the appointment of senior staff. The members of the committee would be elected representatives of the staff, volunteers, consumers of the service and locally elected councillors and the Centre Manager. The Unit or Centre Manager would be responsible to this committee for the implementation of its policies. This arrangement works very well in the Education System with School Governing Committees and there is no reason why it should not work in the form I have proposed for this type of service. This committee would meet once a month and have open access to the Centre clients and staff.

Over the past 10 years community participation in the organising of social services has become just a slogan, the 'in thing'. Much has been written on the subject but there has been very little implementation. Social service workers, like many other professions such as Law and Medicine, have developed mechanisms to justify the exclusion of the lay person from decision making in their area of expertise. To date there has been little participation by clients in the management of services provided by Social Service Departments. Social Service Departments and the social work profession in particular, allow the client to participate at a level which Armstein[22] calls a degree of tokenism; this allows the client to participate by involvement in the consultative process, or by being given information. These two processes, he states, only placate the client.

Writers have drawn attention to this distinction between real client power and forms of tokenism or manipulation.[23] The Barcley Report on the Role and Tasks of Social Workers falls into the trap of recommending this form of client participation. It argues for the feeble concept of allowing clients to take on the advisory role through Local Advisory

Committees. This recommendation was to be expected, it would be difficult to envisage the social work profession behaving differently from the professions such as Law and Medicine it tries to emulate. The report clearly showed that social workers make and take decisions about clients which do not take into account the basic rules of natural justice.

To do this and impede communication is as Freire says "is to reduce men to the status of 'THINGS', and that is a job for the oppressors".[24] Part of the problem is the inbalance in knowledge between the carer and the client. Titmuss pointed this out forceably in 1967.[25] Social workers and Doctors do very little to de-mystify their professions. Indeed social work, by imposing higher and higher academic standards for entry to the profession, are compounding this situation. What information, expertise, training or magic has the social worker which justifies their power to take away the basic natural rights of clients to make decisions about their own lives?

This concept of local and consumer participation is of course different from that put forward by those who argue for 'patch work'. In the experiments reported so far there have been no built in official machinery for the consumer and staff to influence policy. No form of service delivery can function effectively without both staff and consumer participation in some official form. This has been opposed by the social work profession in the past, but all professions must be monitored by the public and consumer.

This approach, however, raises the problem of accountability. It has been pointed out by Bamford[26] that managers of social work have "a responsibility to ensure that the disadvantaged clients ...... receive a fair allocation of resources - will need to resist considerable pressure if they are to achieve fairness in the allocation of resources". The present structure of Social Services Departments, with its leadership by social workers has not so far lived up to his expectations. Social workers as managers have allowed resources to be placed in areas of their own concern, such as children, not in the areas of desperate need, such as services for the elderly. Is this because social workers cannot be objective and allocate resources to fields that they are not interested in? The past performance of social workers in allocating resources must not be allowed to continue. Clients, workers and the local community must be allowed to decide along with staff where finance and manpower is allocated. The decision making process must not be allowed to stay in the hands of professionals but must be shared with others.

My argument is, therefore, that much as domiciliary care is a discipline related to many fields, "so the needs and conditions of older persons are multifaceted, Housing needs are linked to health status and condition, and both, in turn, may be directly related to income level. Service interventions, therefore, require linkages between medical, health, social, environmental and, at times, legal services. One of the primary barriers to the effective provision of services to the elderly is all too often the lack of an organisational approach in bringing together medical, health and social service systems on a co-ordinated and, at times, integrated approach to the needs of the older individual and his family."[27] I hope that my recommendations would go a long way to achieving some of that co-ordination.

The sole purpose of Domiciliary Care should be to give the elderly every assistance in order to ensure that they remain for as long as possible in their own familiar domestic surroundings. Domiciliary Care is only part of a sub-system of social care. To enable the elderly person to enjoy adequate standards, the service must be seen in relation to the allied medical and social security system. A relatively high proportion of elderly persons live just above or on the poverty line. Furthermore, the likelihood of falling below the poverty line increases the longer the old person lives. State pensions and benefits are inadequate but also many old persons do not take up the benefits that they are entitled to. There is much evidence to support this.[28]

All the needs of the elderly originate and develop through interaction with the social and physical environment. The physical environment may impose undue restrictions upon the movement and development of the elderly. Inadequate and inappropriately designed housing or housing built in inappropriate places, all place extra burdens on the elderly and the services that help them. Old people who live in poverty and inadequate housing, shift their level of aspiration downwards in the course of time, until they resign themselves to the impossibility of improving their surroundings. It is not a large step then to physical deterioration and depression.

Diagram 8.2 Organisation of Neighbourhood Support Unit for the Elderly

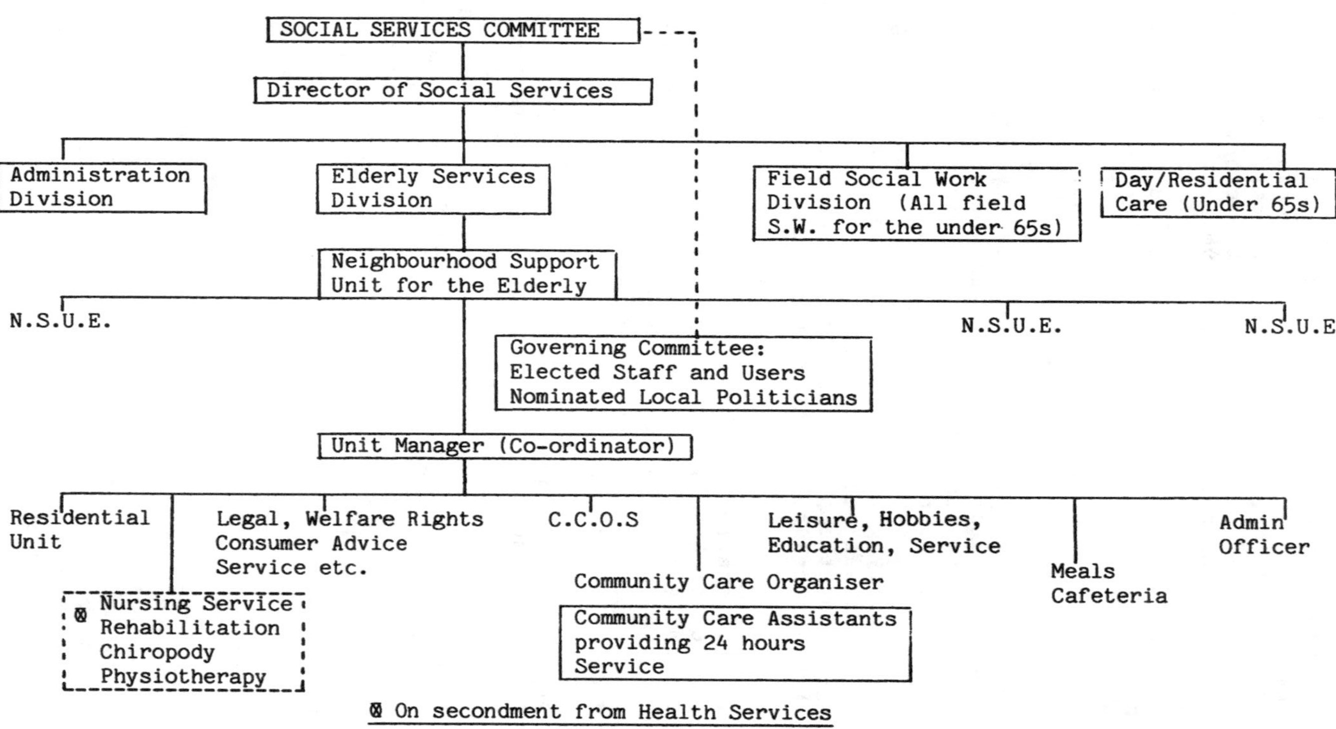

The work of the social and medical services is made that much more difficult if this downward spiral is not halted. All the housing, medical, social services and social security must therefore work in co-operation to provide an effective preventative service.

The concept of demand, which is closely connected with need, should be the starting point for planning and action in the context of social policy. There has never been a national study of the social and medical needs of the elderly. Harris's study of the Handicapped and Impaired in 1971 examined to some extent, the needs of the elderly, but many important questions remain unanswered. What are the needs of the elderly today? What in particular are the different needs of those between 65 and 75, the over 75 and over 85s? How do these needs change as the elderly get older? How, where, and by whom, should these needs be met? Does the increasing ageing of the population make it necessary to expand the services quantitatively or qualitatively?

Summary

In this chapter I have argued that society, and in particular Social Service Departments, have consistently failed to provide adequate support for those elderly who wish to live in their own homes in the community. It is my belief that every elderly person should have the right to enjoy their life in their own homes, with the help and support of the whole community. I also believe that every elderly person should have the right to participate fully, if they wish, in the management planning and policy development of any service they use. The World Health Organisation recognises this right. In the Alma Ata Declaration in 1978 it was stated that "people have the right and duty to participate individually and collectively in the planning and implementing of their health care".[29] This right is often taken to mean that the clients participate only in decision making in relation to their own individual care. However, I see this right to participate in a wider context. Elderly people have a right to be consulted, to be allowed to advise and to manage, on an equal footing, services with professionals. If this right is to be granted (it should be given as a right) then a number of questions need to be asked. Who selects the representatives to serve on management bodies? What is the relationship of the elected or selected representative to the democratically elected local politician?

Who represents the vulnerable clients, such as the severely mentally impaired or elderly confused, who may at times be unable to elect or select their representative?

The elderly represent one of the largest groups on the workload of the social service workers caseload. Despite this they have constantly lost out in the battle for resources. Phillipson in 1982 argued that perhaps one reason for this was the lack of concern by social workers in general about the needs of the elderly.[30] Others have argued that the bureaucratic nature of Social Service Departments allows established groups like social workers to determine the goals of the agency to the detriment of both the agency and the client. Does this apply to social workers who pursue goals in Social Service Departments which militate against the majority user of the service? Any social worker looking to the Barclay Report for guidance on clients' rights, particularly the elderly's, would have his present attitude reinforced. The report says very little about the rights of the elderly but much about the rights of children. This reflects the interests of most social workers.

Resource allocation by both Central and Local Government has not kept in line with the needs of the elderly. The present fiscal climate is very bleak. The failure of Government to implement its policies on community care are evident from the publication of the document 'Care in the Community' in 1981. The document acknowledges that shortages of resources, organisation problems and the attitude of many professionals have hindered the development of the community care policy. As professional groups in Social Services argue for more and more control over their own conduct and the manager perform impossible tasks with little finance, all of this coupled with the increase in the number of elderly persons makes it all the more important that the elderly should have more involvement in policy decision making. If Social Service Staff believe in client self determination they must allow the elderly an equal say in decisions about their own care. As Frederick Ozanam, the founder of one of the largest international social service voluntary organisations, said "My friend, let there not be over much day-dreaming and academic introspection. Let us rescue our studies from the field of empty theorising and vain speculation, let us translate during life our beliefs into deeds".

Notes

1. J. Shaw, *On Our Conscience* (Penguin, London, 1971).

2. E. Goffman, *Asylums: Essays on the Social Situations of Mental Patients and other Inmates* (Doubleday, New York 1961). B. Robb, *Sans Everything* (Nelson, London, 1967). P. Townsend, *The Last Refuge* (Routledge and Kegan Paul, London, 1962).

3. Robb, 'Sans Everything' (1967).

4. Robb, Sans Everything (1967) and Townsend The Last Refuge (1962).

5. R.G. Bennett and I. Nahemow, 'The Relations between Social Isolation, Socialisation and Adjustment in Residents of a Home for the Aged' in M.P. Lawton (ed.), *Proceedings of Institute on Mentally Impaired Aged* (Maurice Jacob Press, Philadelphia, 1965).

6. J. Jenkins, D. Felce, B. Lunt and L. Powell, 'Increasing Engagement in Activity of Residents in Old Peoples Homes by providing Recreational Materials', *Behaviour Research and Therapy*, Vol. 15 (1977).

7. B.A. Yawney and D.L. Slover, 'Relocation of the Elderly', *Social Work*, Vol. 18 (1973).

8. Author's PhD. Research - Sheffield University.

9. C. Godlove, L. Richard and G. Rodwell, *Time for Action*, Joint Unit for Social Services Research (University of Sheffield, Sheffield, 1982).

10. P. Chapman, *Unmet Needs and the Delivery of Care*, Occasional Papers on Social Administration, No. 61 (Bedford Square Press, London, 1979).

11. D. Plank, *Caring for the Elderly* (Greater London Council, 1977) and P. Chapman, *Unmet Needs*. A. Harris, *Social Welfare for the Elderly* (HMSO, London, 1968) and Hunt, *The Home Help Service in England and Wales* (HMSO, London, 1970).

12. O.P.C.S., *General Household Survey 1980* (HMSO, London, 1982).

13. Report of the Committee on Local Authority and Allied Personal Social Services (1969) HMSO, Cmd. 3703. E. Goldberg, *Helping the Aged* (George Allen and Unwin, London, 1971). J. Neill, 'Reactions to Integration', *Social Work Today*, Vol. 4 (1 Nov. 1973). P. Parsloe and O. Stevenson, *Social Service Teams: The Practitioners View* (HMSO, London, 1978). B.A.S.W. Guidelines 'Social Work with the Elderly' *Social Work Today*, Vol. 8 (12 April 1977). B.A.S.W. Guidelines (12 April 1977).

14. T. Bamford, *Managing Social Work* (Tavistock Publications, London, 1982).

15. See R. Hadley and M. McGrath (eds.), *Going Local* (Bedford Square Press/NVCO, London, 1980).

16. E. Goldberg and R.W. Warburton, *Ends and Means in Social Work* (George Allen and Unwin, London, 1979).

17. E. Goldberg and N. Connelly, *The Effectiveness of Social Care for the Elderly* (Heinemann Educational Books, London, 1982).

18. A. Hey, 'Providing Basic Services at Home', in *Organising Social Service Departments* (Heinemann, London, 1980).

19. D. Challis and B. Davis, 'A new approach to Community Care for the Elderly', *Br. J. Social Work*, Vol. 10 (1980).

20. Author's PhD. Research, Sheffield University.

21. P. Barcley, *Social Workers: Their Role and Tasks* (Bedford Square Press, London, 1982).

22. S. Arnstein, A Ladder of Citizen Participation, *Journal of American Institute of Planners*, Vol. 6 (1977).

23. C. Cockburn, *The Local State: Management of Cities and People* (Pluto Press, London, 1977).

24. P. Freire, *Pedagogy of the Oppressed* (Penguin, Harmondsworth, 1970).

25. R.M. Titmuss, *Choice and the Welfare State: Commitment to Welfare* (George Allen and Unwin, London, 1968).

26. T. Bamford, *Managing Social Work*.

27. W.M. Beattie, 'Ageing and the Social Services', in R.H. Binstock and E. Sharas (eds.), *Handbook of Ageing and the Social Sciences* (Van Nos. Reinhold, New York, 1976).

28. N. Hurwitz, *British Medical Journal*, p.536 (1969).

29. World Health Organisation, Primary Health Care, Alma Ata, World Health Organisation, Geneva (1978).

30. C. Phillipson, *Capitalism and the Construction of Old Age* (The Macmillan Press Ltd, London, 1982).

INDEX

For Product Safety Concerns and Information please contact our EU representative GPSR@taylorandfrancis.com
Taylor & Francis Verlag GmbH, Kaufingerstraße 24, 80331 München, Germany

www.ingramcontent.com/pod-product-compliance
Lightning Source LLC
Chambersburg PA
CBHW050440280326
41932CB00013BA/2189

* 9 7 8 1 0 3 2 7 3 2 7 0 1 *